ELFANDE

CONTACT
ILLUSTRATION

TWENTY FOURTH
EDITION

Publisher
Nick Gould

Published by Elfande Ltd
Surrey House, 31 Church Street
Leatherhead, Surrey KT22 8EF

Tel: + 44 (0)1372 220 330
Fax: + 44 (0)1372 220 340
Email: mail@contact-uk.com
Web: www.contact-uk.com

Contact 24 Illustration
ISBN No: 1-905727-13-5
(13 digit): 978-1-905727-13-1

Sales
Wendy Ray • Anne Gould

Financial Director
Val Crabtree

Finance
Julia Collyer

Book Production, Web & Online Services
Suzy Woolston • Dave Millar

Book details
Typeset in Contact type family
designed exclusively for Elfande Ltd
by Alan Rimmer: www.fatchair.com
Printed and bound in China
through World Print Ltd, Hong Kong
Required scanning and retouching by CONTACT

Front Cover
Kerry Roper, pages 296-297

Welcome to
CONTACT 24

Image by Sarah Coleman (pages 212–213)

Contact 24 is your ultimate tool for sourcing the illustrators for your next job. The printed pages of this book present a wide range of illustration styles and subject matter.

Our unique thumbnail category sections allow you to find artists of specific expertise and the online portfolio each illustrator has on our site gives you the opportunity to view a further 20 images from each artist.

The online electronic version of the book puts you in touch directly with click through email and web addresses as well as links from the thumbnail sections.

Our handy pocket edition of the book is also available – very useful for taking to client meetings.

We think that Contact 24 gives you an all round tool for sourcing and hope that you enjoy browsing the book in its many forms.

Remember to tell advertisers that you found them through CONTACT.

Enjoy!

Check it out: www.contactEbooks.com

Quick reference categorised index

The quick reference section is located before the main index and uses thumbnails of images from the pages to create the quick reference categories. The purpose of this thumbnail index is as a guide for when you are looking for an illustrator skilled in specific subjects, certain styles or using particular media. For example, if you require someone who does figurative work, turn to pages 382–384 and look through the thumbnail images – all by illustrators who specialise in this area. Under each thumbnail image is the name of the illustrator and their page number. Once you see a style that you like, turn directly to that illustrator's page to see more of their work and their full contact details. In the E-Book, you can click on the thumbnail image to be taken straight through to their main page on-screen.

CONTACT 24 on the web

www.contactEbooks.com

Contact is on the web in several forms. The newest of these is our E-Book where you can view every page in the printed edition in its entirety online. Each email and web address on a page works as a live-link. You can zoom into particular areas of a page for a close-up look and also print out pages for reference. In addition pages can be emailed to colleagues for collaboration of ideas. The thumbnail category index described opposite is fully linked in the online version, so having found a certain image you can access the illustrator's contact details with one click. Likewise the index pages link from name to main page. As the market requirements have changed, so too has the need for new skills both screen and print based. In the E-Book you can find links to animation and showreels from some pages.

www.contactacreative.com

Our well-established portfolio website is an extension of the book and presents a further 20 images for each artist along with contact details and a biography. The site can be used to find specific or broad subject matter in either illustration, photography or both by using the different levels of search criteria. The simplest way to use this site is to use any of the www.contact-me.net web addresses located within the contributors' details for immediate access.

To broaden its appeal the portfolio site has been extended to include the work of a range of photographic services that assist in the photographic industry such as studios for hire, location finders and stylists.

www.contactbooks.com

Historical copies of the books remain on our website indefinitely should you wish to look up an old image. If the contributor is a current advertiser you can find up to date contact details with their online portfolio or you can phone us.

Image (far left) by Cameron Law (page 96)
image (left) by Gary Neill (pages 350-351)

CONTACT

T *Telephone*
F *Fax*
M *Mobile*
T/F *Telephone/Fax*
E *Email*
W *Web Address*

CONTENTS

Janette Bornmarker

Stora Nygatan 44
S–111 27 Stockholm
Sweden

T *+ 46 (0)8 222 224*
M *+ 46 (0)733 307 398*
E *janette@jaboillustration.se*
W *www.jaboillustration.se*
W *www.contact-me.net/JanetteBornmarker*

Paul Morton

Hot Frog Graphics • Illustration & Design
UK

☎ + 44 (0)1226 242 777
📱 + 44 (0)7949 718 466
✉ hotfroggraphics@blueyonder.co.uk
🌐 www.hotfroggraphics.com
🌐 http://hotfroggraphics.blogspot.com
🌐 www.contact-me.net/PaulMorton

See also Contacts 13–23

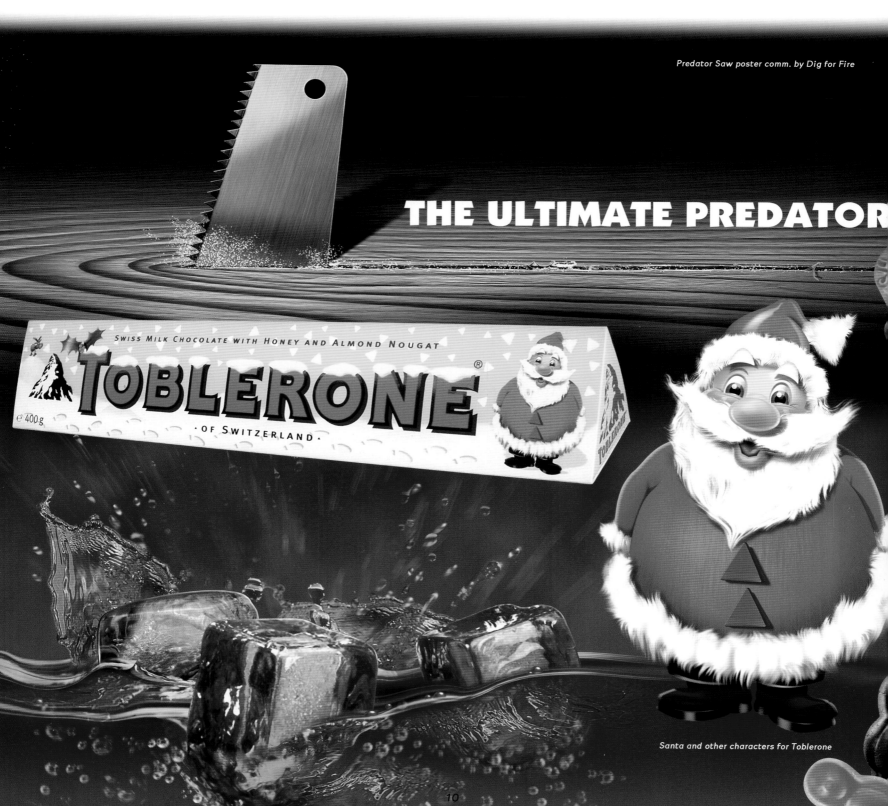

Predator Saw poster comm. by Dig for Fire

Santa and other characters for Toblerone

Jon Higham

4 Prospect Cottages
Caldbec Hill
Battle
East Sussex TN33 OJR
UK

☎ + 44 (0)1424 772 173
📱 + 44 (0)7817 873 513
✉ jonhigham@mac.com
🌐 www.jonhigham.co.uk
🌐 www.contact-me.net/JonHigham

Clients include:
Sainsbury's, Nestlé, BBC Worldwide
(Cbeebies magazine), paperchase,
The Leith Agency, Twizler Cards,
John Brown Junior, Michael O'Mara,
gratterpalm.

For more examples see Contact 21,
22, 23.

Marc Arundale

169a Bedford Hill
London SW12 9HG
UK

T + 44 (0)20 8673 1449
E marc.arundale@talk21.com
W www.contact-me.net/MarcArundale
W www.marcArundaleillustration.homestead.com

I'm a London based illustrator working for the last number of years in image making, montage, photography, multimedia and general design, mainly for editorial, publishing and advertising clients.

Clients include:
Radio Times, The Guardian, The Times, Mail on Sunday, The Telegraph, Aladdin Books, Macmillan Books, Random House, John Brown Publishing, BBH, TBWA/GGT, PPL, Brand X, Digital Vision/Getty Images, Gasoline, Carlton & Gibson cards, Sainsbury's, Paperchase, Furry Records, Brass Tacks and Dennis, IPC, Haymarket, Reed, Centaur, National Magazines, VNU, BBC, UKIP, Xbox and Emap magazines.

Rob Hefferan

11 Camwood Fold
Clayton-Le-Woods
Chorley
Lancashire PR6 7SD
UK

☎ + 44 (0)1772 337 103
Ⓜ + 44 (0)7811 359 345
Ⓔ robhefferan@yahoo.co.uk
Ⓦ www.robhefferan.net
Ⓦ www.contact-me.net/RobHefferan

Please see all my work at
www.robhefferan.net

Also see previous Contact Illustrators
books for further examples of my work,
brochure available on request.

Christopher Jasper Rainham

Acre House
Kiln Lane
Milnrow
Rochdale OL16 3TR
UK

T + 44 (0)1706 868 577
M + 44 (0)7786 686 776
E administrator@christopherrainham.co.uk
W www.christopherrainham.co.uk
W www.contact-me.net/ChristopherRainham

On the dizzy edge

Thistles and vinegar

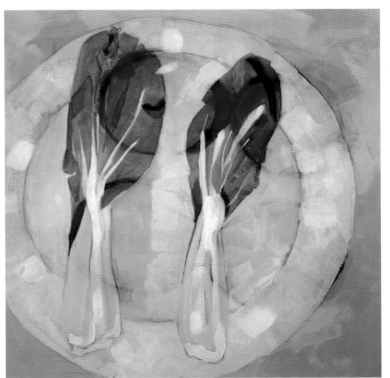

Pak choi

Cocktail

Ben Morris

Edinburgh
UK

☎/📠 + 44 (0)131 332 7307
📱 + 44 (0)7880 574 658
✉ benmorris@benmorrisillustration.com
🌐 www.benmorrisillustration.com
🌐 www.contact-me.net/BenMorris

Clients include:
Doctor Who Magazine,
Reuters, E-on,
Radio Times, BBC Education,
Forestry Commission,
Property Ladder Magazine,
WHSmith, Which? Magazine.

See also Contact 15 page 16,
Contact 16 page 16, Contact 17
page 27, Contact 18 page 17,
Contact 19 page 19, Contact 20
page 15, Contact 21 page 15,
Contact 22 page 13 and
Contact 23 page 14.

Ben Morris

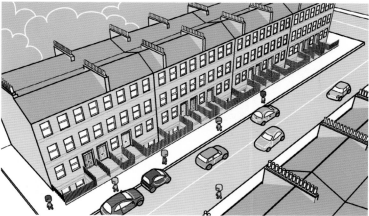

Nadolig Llawen!

clydebank

Matt Murphy

Lorna
Coldharbour
Sherborne
Dorset DT9 4AH
UK

☎ + 44 (0)1935 817 751
📱 + 44 (0)7876 593 841
✉ matt@blackcoffeeproject.com
🌐 www.blackcoffeeproject.com
🌐 www.contact-me.net/MattMurphy

Client list :
The New York Times Magazine, Time Warner Books, Prospect Magazine, The Big Issue, The Observer, The Sunday Telegraph, The Independent on Sunday, New Scientist, Wieden + Kennedy, Transworld Publishers, FMX, Redwood Group, Time Out, The Independent, The Independent on Sunday, Country Life, Leagas Delaney, Pagewise, Pulse, Reader's Digest.

Images taken from the book 'The Genie in the Bottle'
written by Hugh Montgoomery, art directed and designed by Monica Bratt at Pagewise.

Paul Garland

UK

☎ + 44 (0)7761 136 314
✉ paul@pgarland.com
🌐 www.pgarland.com
🌐 www.contact-me.net/PaulGarland

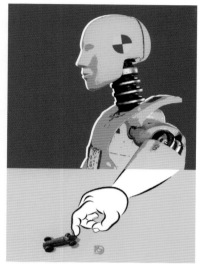

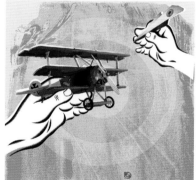

Alan Baker

St Michael's
Telscombe Village
Near Lewes
East Sussex BN7 3HZ
UK

☎ + 44 (0)1273 302 333
✉ info@alanbakeronline.com
🌐 www.mywholeportfolio.com/AlanBaker
🌐 www.contact-me.net/AlanBaker

What to do with my text space?
Draw in it?   ^^^^^
No…That's not allowed.   O--O
Tell you how brilliant I am?   ..
No… You can see that.   __
Spell it out in Morse?
-- .- -.-- -... .   -. --- -
The basic problem in marketing, is one
of exploration, and a determination to
go on genuinely trying to put your
name and service/product across.

```
ALANBAKERALANBAKERALANBAKE
LANBAKERALANBAKERALANBAKERA
ANBAKERALANBAKERALANBAKERAL
NBAKERALANBAKERALANBAKERALA
BAKERALANBAKERALANBAKERALAN
AKERALANBAKERALANBAKERALAN
KERALANBAKERALANBAKERALAN
ERALANBAKERALANBAKERALANBA
RALANBAKERALANBAKERALANBAKE
ALANBAKERALANBAKERALANBAKER
LANBAKERALANBAKERALANBAKER
```

Gary Bullock

Bullock Barn
16 Alford Gardens
Myddle, Shrewsbury
Shropshire SY4 3RG
UK

T + 44 (0)1939 291 646
F + 44 (0)1939 291 645
M + 44 (0)7860 214 253
E garybullock@btinternet.com
W www.bullockillustration.com

Also represented by 'Three In A Box Inc'
T + 44 (0)20 8853 1236

All work on this page produced in 'Illustrator'. Please don't hesitate to contact me if you have a query or wish to discuss a quote.

Further samples can be seen on my website www.bullockillustration.com

See also Contact 14–23.

Recent clients have included: Shell, GM Motors, Sainsbury's, Mercedes-Benz, BP, Nissan, Tesco, Co-op, Asda, Royal Bank of Canada, Hershey, Greater Manchester Police, Ontario State Lottery, Hasbro, GB Airways, Coca-Cola, Coors, Which? Magazine, OUP, TV Times.

Hemesh Alles

124 Princes Avenue
Gunnersbury Park Estate
London W3 8LT
UK

☎ + 44 (0)20 8752 0159
✉ hemesh.alles@virgin.net
🌐 www.contact-me.net/HemeshAlles

Style of work: realistic figurative in watercolour, black and white line and line and wash.

I also do cartoon style illustrations for children's books and audio books.

Clients: Orion Children's Books, Naxos Audio Books, Scholastic Ltd, Harcourt Educational, Kingfisher Publications, Ginn, Templar Publishing, Oxford University Press, Cambridge University Press, Harper Collins, Watts Publishing, Weidenfeld & Nicholson amongst others.

PEACE · ON · EARTH

Sandra Howgate

London
UK

☎ + 44 (0)7729 529 530
✉ info@sandrahowgate.com
🌐 www.sandrahowgate.com
🌐 www.contact-me.net/SandraHowgate

Clients include: Penguin, Random House, Hamlyn, Nestlé, The Royal College of Psychiatrists, The Commission for Racial Equality, News International, Lexis Nexis, Emap, Redwood, McMillan Scott, Surestart, The Independent, The Guardian.

Please see my website for more images, as well as page 19 of Contact 22.

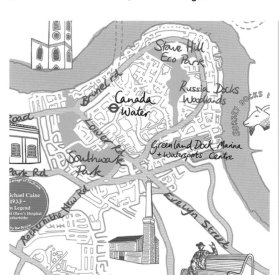

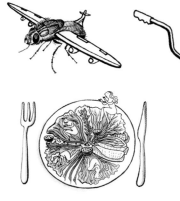

Janice Nicolson

75 Quebec Drive
East Kilbride
Glasgow G75 8SE
UK

☎ + 44 (0)1355 223 631
📱 + 44 (0)7791 504 664
✉ janicenicolson@btinternet.com
🌐 www.contact-me.net/JaniceNicolson

For further examples of my work
please see
Contact 13 page 10
Contact 14 page 442
Contact 15 page 25
Contact 16 page 53

I can supply all these pages.

Andy Hunt

UK

T + 44 (0)1566 785 534
M + 44 (0)7870 336 393
E andyhtoons@clara.co.uk
W www.andyhunt.com
W www.contact-me.net/AndyHunt

Kate Taylor

UK

☎ + 44 (0)1274 676 870
✉ kate@yorkshiregirl.freeserve.co.uk
🌐 www.contact-me.net/KateTaylor

Further samples in Contact 12–23.

David Holmes

5 Calvert Street
Primrose Hill
London NW1 8NE
UK

T + 44 (0)20 7586 0363
F + 44 (0)20 7586 8907
M + 44 (0)7976 872 377
E david@cecilholmes.demon.co.uk
W www.contact-me.net/DavidHolmes

Joy Gosney

4 White Street
Brighton BN2 OJH
UK

☎ + 44 (0)1273 603 482
📱 + 44 (0)7721 622 652
✉ joy@joygosney.co.uk
🌐 www.joygosney.co.uk
🌐 www.contact-me.net/JoyGosney

Please visit my website to see the full range of my work, including book jackets, advertising, food and drink, lettering and children's portfolio.

Also see
Contact 23 pg. 17
Contact 20 pg. 172
Contact 19 pg. 187

Recent clients include:
Harper Collins, Transworld, The London Aquarium, The South Bank Centre, Condé Nast Traveller, Brown Thomas (Ireland), The First Post (internet newspaper), Ebury, Leeds University, The Guardian.

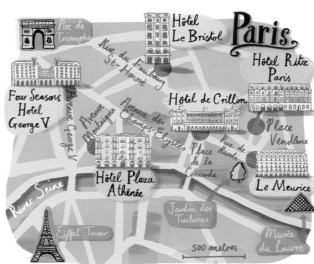

Emily Bolam

24 Vine Street
Brighton
BN1 4AG
UK

T *+ 44 (0)1273 622 991*
E *emily.bolam@virgin.net*
W *www.emilybolam.com*
W *www.contact-me.net/EmilyBolam*

Colin Shelbourn

Pine Howe
Helm Road
Windermere
Cumbria LA23 2NL
UK

T *+ 44 (0)1539 442 052*
M *+ 44 (0)7779 77 53 56*
E *c@rtoonist.com*
W *www.shelbourn.com*
W *www.contact-me.net/ColinShelbourn*

Thanks to Contact 23, another successful year producing cartoon illustrations for publishing, advertising, education and business.

Cheers to all my clients, old, new and potential... your very good 'elf.

Julie Clough

10 Grange Park Road
Cheadle
Cheshire
SK8 1HQ
UK

T + 44 (0)161 428 8755
M + 44 (0)7966 466 883
E ju@julieclough.co.uk
W www.contact-me.net/JulieClough

Ellis Nadler

PO Box 4DY
London W1A 4DY
UK

T + 44 (0)845 053 1620
F + 44 (0)870 163 9649
E info@nadler.co.uk
W www.nadler.co.uk
W www.contact-me.net/EllisNadler

I have many years of experience working with clients in advertising, design, publishing and editorial. Artwork delivered on budget and on time. See previous Contact books for more images.

Max Ellis

UK

UK agent

CIA
36 Wellington Street
Covent Garden
London WC2E 7BD
UK

US agent

Bernstein & Andriulli
58 West 40th Street
New York NY 10018
USA

M + 44 (0)7976 242 378
E max@junkyard.co.uk
W www.junkyard.co.uk
W www.contact-me.net/MaxEllis

T + 44 (0)20 7240 8925
F + 44 (0)20 7836 1177
E info@centralillustration.com

T + 1 212 682 1490
T + 1 212 286 1890
E louisa@ba-reps.com

Murray Heath

16 Coldharbour
Uffculme
Cullompton
Devon EX15 3EE
UK

T *+ 44 (0)1884 841 624*
M *+ 44 (0)7834 455 556*
E *murray@soulplanet.org*
W *www.soulplanet.org*
W *www.contact-me.net/MurrayHeath*

Debbie Clark

13 Carline Road
Lincoln
Lincolnshire LN1 1HL
UK

T + 44 (0)1522 543 250
M + 44 (0)7939 292 089
E debbie@debbieclark.eu
W www.contact-me.net/DebbieClark

Illustration and character
development. Digital and traditional.
Extensive client list on request. CONTACT

Pete Ellis

Drawgood Illustration
22 Manwood Road
London SE4 1AD
UK

T + 44 (0)20 8690 5013
M + 44 (0)7960 447 604
E pete@drawgood.com
W www.drawgood.com
W www.contact-me.net/PeteEllis

UK Agent

Meiklejohn Illustration
5 Risborough Street
London SE1 OHF
UK

T + 44 (0)20 7593 0500
W www.meiklejohn.co.uk

Andrew Hennessey

24 Westfield Way
Ruislip
Middlesex
HA4 6HN
UK

M + 44 (0)7798 688 530
E andrewhennessey@blueyonder.co.uk
W www.andrewhennessey.com
W www.ahennessey.co.uk
W www.contact-me.net/AndrewHennessey

Digital illustration for advertising, character design, children's book publishing, online games and websites.

More of my work can be found in Contact 17–23.

Recent clients include:

M&C Saatchi, Momentum, BBC, Walkers, Virgin, Chad Valley, Halfords, Macmillan, Harcourt Publishing and Pearson Education.

County Studio International Ltd

The Ginn Stables
Coleorton
Leicestershire
LE67 8FL
UK

T + 44 (0)1530 222 260
F + 44 (0)1530 222 127
E dud@countystudio.com
W www.countystudio.com
W www.contact-me.net/CountyStudio

County Studio provides a creative eye to anyone's needs, with a team of highly experienced illustrators, designers and paper engineers.

We can create concepts through to the finished product, from children's books through to paper engineering and electronic models, packaging or any other requirements.

Inspired by excellence!

David Axtell

4 Park View Terrace
Wadebridge
Cornwall
PL27 7PS
UK

T *+ 44 (0)1208 813 750*
E *davidaxtellillustrator@hotmail.com*
W *www.contact-me.net/DavidAxtell*

The Last Supper

Angelina

Wholesalers of Spitalfields

Industrial Art Studio

Contact: Roger Full
Industrial Art Studio
Consols, St Ives
Cornwall TR26 2HW
UK

☎ + 44 (0)1736 797 651
✉ roger@ind-art.co.uk
🌐 www.ind-art.co.uk
🌐 www.contact-me.net/IndustrialArtStudio

Specialising in conception, creation and production of all forms of high quality technical, product and architectural illustrations and animations for advertising, marketing, exhibition, training and visual communications.

If you can imagine it – we can create it! View over 60 examples of illustration and animation in our galleries at www.ind-art.co.uk

Visible Solutions
to
Invisible Problems

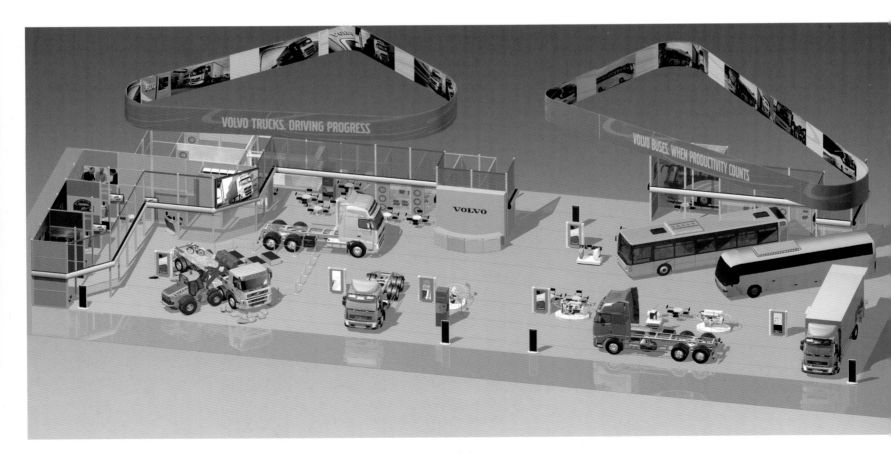

Martin Handford

c/o Elfande Ltd
UK

☎ + 44 (0)1372 220 330
🌐 www.contact-me.net/Martin Handford

I specialise in illustrating crowd scenes, usually with a humorous content. My work has been commissioned for various clients including magazines, newspapers, book publishers and design groups.

Illustration commissioned by 'The Radio Times'

Georgios Manoli

London
UK

M *+ 44 (0)7989 139 492*
E *info@manoli.co.uk*
W *www.manoli.co.uk*
W *www.contact-me.net/GeorgiosManoli*

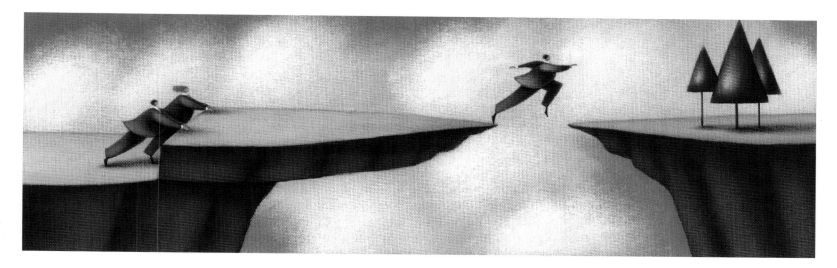

Mike Ritchie

West Barn
Great Whittington
Newcastle upon Tyne
NE19 2HA
UK

☎ + 44 (0)1434 672 461
✉ mr2web@ndirect.co.uk
🌐 www.contact-me.net/MikeRitchie

Specialist areas:
Historical reconstructions, cutaways,
maps and aerial views for print and
interpretive panels.

Picture caption:
Burma – Client: Illustrated London
News Group for Orient-Express Hotels

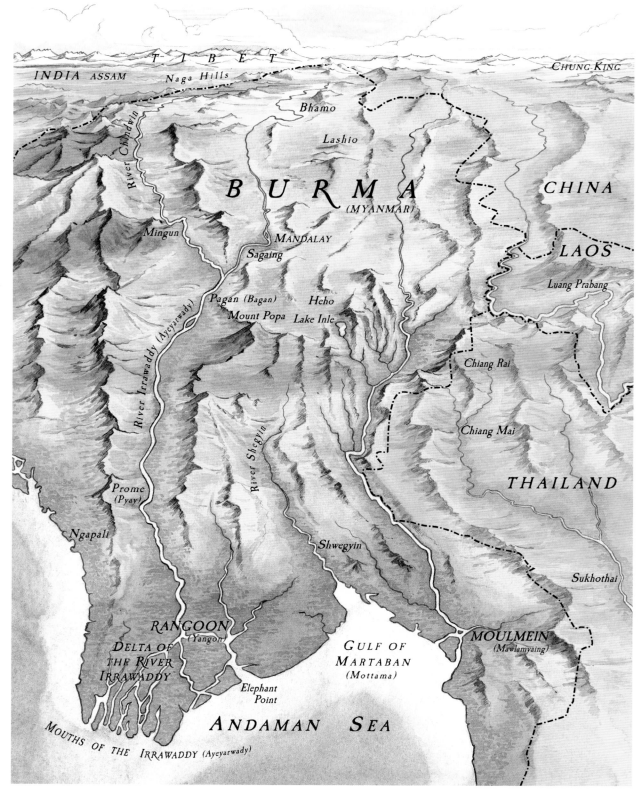

Jane Massey

45 Cranmer Avenue
Hove
East Sussex
BN3 7JP
UK

📞 + 44 (0)1273 710 662
📱 + 44 (0)7891 438 564
✉ massey.design@virgin.net
🌐 www.contact-me.net/JaneMassey

Previous clients include:
Random House, Scholastic,
Campbell Books, Little Tiger Press,
Michael O'Mara Books, Paperchase,
Marks & Spencer plc, Whittards,
John Lewis Partnership, AOL,
Waterstones, ASDA, Ogilvy/Huggies,
WARL/Fairy and Cadbury's.

For more examples please see
Contact 13–22.

Creative Eye Illustration

The Old Bakehouse
3 Church View
Bampton
Oxfordshire OX18 2NE
UK

☎ + 44 (0)1993 851 408
📱 + 44 (0)7770 834 017
✉ info@creativeeye.net
🌐 www.creativeeye.net
🌐 www.contact-me.net/CreativeEye

With over 17 years freelance experience, Mike Renwick services both national and international clients.

Based in Oxfordshire, recent clients have included Toshiba, Halfords, Hunters, Norwich Union Healthcare, Duerr's, Oxford University Press, Dunlopillo, Forward Group, Ocean Spray, Kidde, McVities, Yamaha, Sainsbury's to name but a few.

Advertising, packaging, editorial, press or info graphics. Whether you have a definite project in mind or simply require a quote and examples for a pitch then please contact me.

Further examples can be viewed on my websites. Creative Eye Illustration is not an agency, all the work has been produced by Mike.

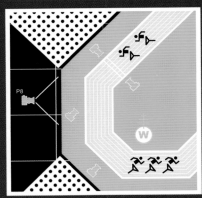

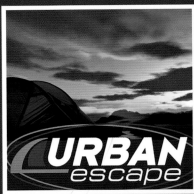

l.y.h.d
let your
hair
down
ceramic straighteners

PHOTOVOLTAIC PANELS
FACING SOUTH
HEAT RECOVERY UNIT
ATRIUM
GRASS/TURF ROOF
ROOF VENTS
OPEN PLAN
RECYCLING BINS
CENTRAL DEPOT
THERMAL MASS
CHILLED BEAMS/ LOW
ENERGY COOLING

RECYCLING
CENTRE
I.T.
comm
FIRTREE
JUNIOR SCHOOL

St. Luke's Hospital

TOWN HALL
TEMPLE
SOLICITORS

SBC
DISTRIBUTION

CLB BANK

ARGUS
Roots
RJ
Sports

AMBULANCE

TOSHIBA
Leading Innovation »
TOSHIBA
Shh...Shelters
Shh...Shelters

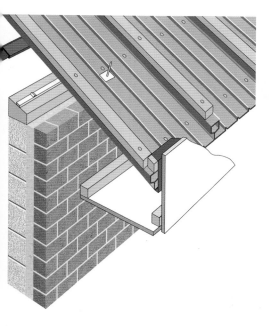

Mike Renwick

E info@creativeeye.net

Flash animated version at www.hi-mag.com/town

Bryan Holdaway

Flat 4 Littleheath
St. Marys Road
Swanley
Kent BR8 7BU
UK

T + 44 (0)1322 615 017
M + 44 (0)7958 795 606
E bryanholdaway@talktalk.net
W www.contact-me.net/BryanHoldaway

I specialise in digital illustration, working in a variety of styles and on a wide range of subject matter.

Derek Matthews

Langhurst Cottage
Prestwick Lane
Chiddingfold
Surrey GU8 4XP
UK

T + 44 (0)1428 684 580
F + 44 (0)1428 685 591
E derekmatthews@btinternet.com
W www.derekmatthews.co.uk
W www.contact-me.net/DerekMatthews

Top notch image creation,
character design and illustration...

Caroline Tomlinson

London
UK

☎ + 44 (0)20 8679 8898
📱 + 44 (0)7709 769 331
✉ info@carolinetomlinson.com
🌐 www.carolinetomlinson.com
🌐 www.contact-me.net/CarolineTomlinson

Clients include: Adventis Group, Caspian Publishing, Contact Magazine, Inside Track Magazine, Meredith Publishing NYC, More Magazine NYC, Myrmidon Publishers, Red Active, Redwood Publishing, Royal Mail, The Coningsby Gallery, The Guardian, The Home Office, Transmission Magazine, Tomorrow London and Wieden & Kennedy.

For further examples of my work see Contact 22 page 92 and Contact 23 page 74.

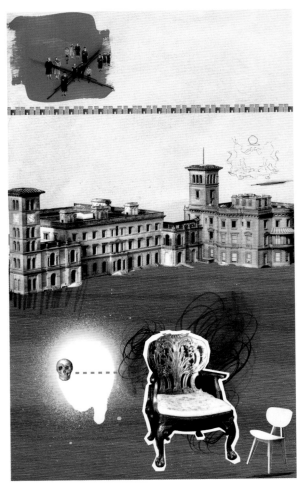

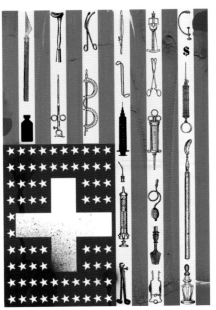

www.fruitman.com

UK

Ⓦ www.fruitman.com
Ⓦ www.contact-me.net/Fruitman

At Fruitman.com you will find extensive
collections of fruit images. You can
select from many different orientations
of many different fruits and use them
as building blocks to create your own
custom compositions.

Ronald Kurniawan

Début Art & The Coningsby Gallery
30 Tottenham Street
London W1T 4RJ
UK

☎ + 44 (0)20 7636 1064
☎ + 44 (0)20 7636 7478
📠 + 44 (0)20 7580 7017
✉ info@debutart.com
🌐 www.debutart.com

I see giant eyed octopuses, little gorillas, big cowboy hats and when people talk, you could see the words coming out of their mouths. Graduated from Art Center College of Design with honours, which makes me special in my Mom's eyes. I was also voted "most classy" in high school. Chah–Ching. Worked for so many companies and magazines, made everyone look good and had fun doing it. I live in a sleepy town called Los Angeles.

Previous clients incl: Dreamworks, Microsoft, MIT, Sony, Mattel Inc., Disney, Village Voice, New York Times, Warner Bros., Esquire Mag., Wired Mag., Men's Health Mag., Technology Review Mag.

I have an extensive portfolio of work online at www.debutart.com

the coningsby gallery

'CMYK World' Comm. by McCann–Erickson for Microsoft Zune.

'Best of LA'. Cover image for LA Weekly.

'Buffoon on AN Island'. (Roq la Rue Gallery Private Collection).

'Postal Service'. Comm. by Wired Magazine.

'Dangerous C'. In The Drawing Club's Private Collection.

'The Type of Man'. Tech Review for MIT about how humans can talk and animals cannot.

'Literary Hoaxes'. Comm. by LA Weekly.

Miles Cole

74 Engel Park
Mill Hill
London
NW7 2HP
UK

T + 44 (0)20 8349 3364
M + 44 (0)7970 746 781
E milesc@dircon.co.uk
W www.milesc.dircon.co.uk
W www.contact-me.net/MilesCole

Experienced illustrator working in editorial, advertising, publishing and design.

Clients include:
Nickleodeon, ITN, General Medical Council, Strathclyde University, Dow Jones Ltd, Macmillan Books, South West Airlines (US), Alliance & Leicester, Wall St Journal, Financial Times, Mail on Sunday,

The Daily Telegraph, The Independent, The Spectator, Investors Chronicle, The Economist, Esquire, Press Gazette, Emap, Times Newspapers, Which? and many more.

Nick Hardcastle

April Cottage
The Rosery
Mulbarton
Norwich NR14 8AL
UK

☎ + 44 (0)1508 570 153
📱 + 44 (0)7973 144 696
✉ nickhardcastle@supanet.com
🌐 www.nickhardcastle.co.uk
🌐 www.contact-me.net/NickHardcastle

I work in pen and ink and also watercolour. My work ranges from the very figurative to detailed architectural and realistic work.

Other work can be seen in Contact no's 19, 20, 21, 22 and 23.

Here are some of my more recent clients:
Templar Publishing, Pearson Education Limited, Oxford University Press, Folio Society, English Heritage, Esquire, Maynard Malone.

"Murderous Minds" book cover published by The Folio Society.

Copyright Nick Hardcastle image taken from the Explorer's Library: The Story of an Aviator. Published by Templar Publishing ISBN 978-1-84011-489-8

Sherlock Holmes "Sign of Four" published by Oxford University Press.

Gordon Hurden Illustration

32 St Davids Hill
Exeter
Devon EX4 4DT
UK

T + 44 (0)1392 435 114
M + 44 (0)7768 110 819
E gordon@gordonhurden.co.uk
W www.gordonhurden.co.uk
W www.contact-me.net/GordonHurden

Illustration for advertising, design,
corporate, publishing and healthcare.

See also: Contact 17 page 161,
Contact 18 page 363,
Contact 19 page 36,
Contact 20 page 55,
Contact 21 page 395,
Contact 23 page 262/263.

Also view: www.gordonhurden.co.uk

Clients include:
British Airways, Britvic Soft Drinks,
Boots, Which?, Debenhams,
Marks & Spencer, Foster's, Green King,
BT Redcare Security, Fox's, Cadbury,
WHSmith, Pedigree, Homepride, Shell,
House of Fraser, Canon, Starburst,
Wedel, Efes, Sainsbury's, Summerfield,
Carlsberg, Blue Cross Hospital,
Guinness, Taylors.

Jacky Rough

142 Gledhow Wood Road
Leeds LS8 1PF
UK

☎ + 44 (0)113 266 7985
✉ jackyrough@aol.com
🌐 www.contact-me.net/JackyRough

For stylised illustrations using
different media suitable for many
applications. I am a member of the
Association of Illustrators and have
appeared in past Contact books.

Christina K

Début Art & The Coningsby Gallery
30 Tottenham Street
London W1T 4RJ
UK

T + 44 (0)20 7636 1064
T + 44 (0)20 7636 7478
F + 44 (0)20 7580 7017
E info@debutart.com
W www.debutart.com

Christina's unique freehand style has been attracting clients in advertising, book publishing and magazine editorial worldwide.

Previous clients include:
La Perla, Levi's, Hot Wheels, Elle Magazine, Defected Records, The Sunday Times, Hint Magazine, HarperCollins Publishers (NY), Men's Health Magazine, Scarlet Magazine, Homes & Gardens Magazine, AXM, Rafael Lopez.

A full portfolio of Christina's work can be reviewed on-line at www.debutart.com

the coningsby gallery

Personal piece.

For Orange Dot.
Fashion illustration exhibition.

For Lectra. Fashion illustration for POS use by a French fashion house.

For Orange Dot.
Fashion illustration exhibition.

Personal piece.

Willie Ryan

Illustration Ltd
2 Brooks Court
Cringle Street
London SW8 5BX
UK

T + 44 (0)20 7720 5202
F + 44 (0)20 7720 5920
E team@illustrationweb.com
W www.mywholeportfolio.com/WillieRyan
W www.contact-me.net/WillieRyan

Representatives in: USA, France, Deutschland & Singapore.

My hi-resolution portfolio is now available to print from the internet for your immediate presentation.

Illustration

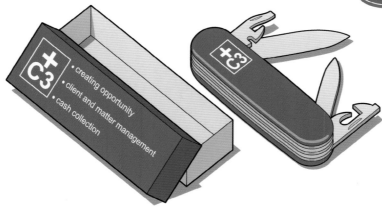

Kenneth Andersson

Stora Nygatan 44
111 27 Stockholm
Sweden

T + 46 (0)87 810 459
M + 46 (0)708 343 742
E info@kennethandersson.com
W www.kennethandersson.com
W www.contact-me.net/KennethAndersson

Agent:
Eye Candy Illustration
Pepperpot Corner, Manor Yard
Blithbury Road
Hamstall Ridware
Staffs WS15 3RS
UK

T + (0)20 8291 0729
E mark@eyecandy.co.uk
W www.eyecandy.co.uk

Kenneth Andersson is based in Stockholm, Sweden. He works with magazines, book publishers and advertising agencies.
Some clients are: The Guardian, Sunday Times Magazine, BBC Radio Times, Random House, Shots Magazine, Newsweek, Dreams That Money Can Buy, Toyota, Alfa Laval, The Swedish Television, The Daily News Magazine, Business Weekly.

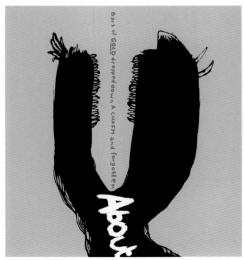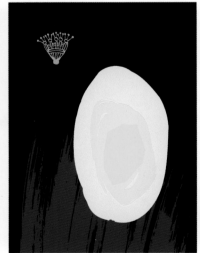

Evelina Frescura

10a Cato Road
London SW4 7TX
UK

T + 44 (0)20 7720 6854
M + 44 (0)7905 397 096
E evi@dircon.co.uk
W www.contact-me.net/EvelinaFrescura

Client list:
Vodafone, Sofitel, ntl,
Air New Zealand, Barclays,
EMI, Adidas, T-Mobile, Biomni,
Yorkshire Water, Graphics
International, British Midlands,
Sainsbury's, Watson Wyatt,
WHSmith, Waitrose.

Daniel Howarth

Advocate
39 Church Road
Wimbledon Village
London SW19 5DQ
UK

T *+ 44 (0)20 8879 1166*
E *mail@advocate-art.com*
W *www.advocate-art.com*
W *www.contact-me.net/DanielHowarth*

The Boy Fitz Hammond

Advocate
39 Church Road
Wimbledon Village
London SW19 5DQ
UK

T + 44 (0)20 8879 1166
E mail@advocate-art.com
W www.advocate-art.com
W www.contact-me.net/FitzHammond

advocate art

Jo Parry

Advocate
39 Church Road
Wimbledon Village
London SW19 5DQ
UK

T + 44 (0)20 8879 1166
E mail@advocate-art.com
W www.advocate-art.com
W www.contact-me.net/JoParry

advocate art

Katie Saunders

Advocate
39 Church Road
Wimbledon Village
London SW19 5DQ
UK

T + 44 (0)20 8879 1166
E mail@advocate-art.com
W www.advocate-art.com
W www.contact-me.net/KatieSaunders

Nick Spender

Advocate
39 Church Road
Wimbledon Village
London SW19 5DQ
UK

T *+ 44 (0)20 8879 1166*
E *mail@advocate-art.com*
W *www.advocate-art.com*
W *www.contact-me.net/NickSpender*

Sarah Horne

Advocate
39 Church Road
Wimbledon Village
London SW19 5DQ
UK

T + 44 (0)20 8879 1166
E mail@advocate-art.com
W www.advocate-art.com
W www.contact-me.net/SarahHorne

advocate art

the WORLD according to RICHARD ROGERS

Simon Mendez

Advocate
39 Church Road
Wimbledon Village
London SW19 5DQ
UK

T *+ 44 (0)20 8879 1166*
E *mail@advocate-art.com*
W *www.advocate-art.com*
W *www.contact-me.net/SimonMendez*

Tom Lane

Advocate
39 Church Road
Wimbledon Village
London SW19 5DQ
UK

T *+ 44 (0)20 8879 1166*
E *mail@advocate-art.com*
W *www.advocate-art.com*
W *www.contact-me.net/TomLane*

advocate art

Tom Percival

Advocate
39 Church Road
Wimbledon Village
London SW19 5DQ
UK

T + 44 (0)20 8879 1166
E mail@advocate-art.com
W www.advocate-art.com
W www.contact-me.net/TomPercival

Phil Phillips   Harmony Clearwater-Phillips   Fred Phillips   Evil Fred   Violet   The Collector

Phil Wrigglesworth

UK

☎ + 44 (0)7939 794 267
✉ phil@philwrigglesworth.com
🌐 www.philwrigglesworth.com
🌐 www.contact-me.net/PhilWrigglesworth

Paul Shorrock

80 Knowsley Road
Wilpshire
Lancashire
BB1 9PN
UK

☎ + 44 (0)1254 243 855
📱 + 44 (0)7961 355 411
✉ shorrock@dircon.co.uk
🌐 www.paulshorrock.com
🌐 www.contact-me.net/PaulShorrock

Clients include:
Astra Zeneca, Atos Origin, BAE Systems, The BBC, BLSW, Bloodaxe Books, Bloomberg, BP, The British Council, CBI, Centaur, Channel 4, Connected, Daily Telegraph, Dennis Publishing, Design Week, The Economist, Esquire, E–Z–Go, FHM, Financial Times, The Guardian, GGT, GQ, Hertz, IBM, The Independent, Langsdale Crook, Macmillan, Mail on Sunday, Marketing Week, Men's Fitness, NHS, National Magazines, NatWest Bank, Observer, PC World, PwC, Readers' Digest, Redwood, RBI, Rieches Baird, Sainsbury's, The Sunday Telegraph, The Sunday Times, The Times, TES, Time magazine, Time Out, Transport and General Workers' Union, Unilever, Which?, WWAV Rapp Collins, YooDoo.

Covers for Data Strategy magazine.

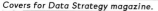

Rich Picture for Atos Origin.

Alex Trochut

Début Art & The Coningsby Gallery
30 Tottenham Street
London W1T 4RJ
UK

☎ + 44 (0)20 7636 1064
☎ + 44 (0)20 7636 7478
📠 + 44 (0)20 7580 7017
✉ info@debutart.com
🌐 www.debutart.com

Alex's unique work is a carefully considered synthesis of illustration, design and, in many instances, letter-form. Alex's work has been attracting a range of leading companies worldwide from the fields of advertising, design and magazine and book publishing.

Previous clients include:
Coca-Cola, British Airways, Universal Music/The Rolling Stones, Bacardi, Esquire Magazine, The Economist, The Guardian.

More examples of Alex's work can be found in his extensive and printable portfolio on the web at www.debutart.com

Comm. by Zip Design for Universal Records.

Personal work.

Poster for Estrella Levante.

Front cover for Beautiful Decay Magazine.

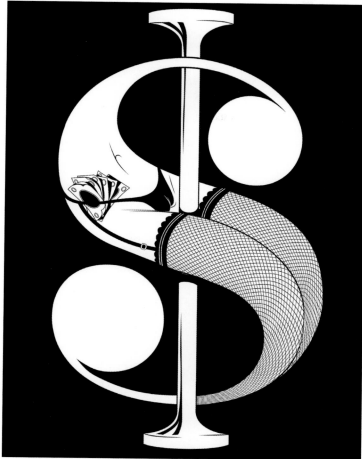

Poster for Acido Surtido Magazine.

Comm. by Computer Arts Magazine for '10 ways to get a Job' feature.

Comm. by Super Expresso for Mosquito Tech parties.

from

NEW YORK return

from

HONGKONG return

from

DUBAI return

Our most attractive prices
at ba.com

 BRITISH AIRWAYS

Comm. by BBH Adv. for British Airways for posters and press.

ilovedust

Début Art & The Coningsby Gallery
30 Tottenham Street
London W1T 4RJ
UK

☎ + 44 (0)20 7636 1064
☎ + 44 (0)20 7636 7478
🖷 + 44 (0)20 7580 7017
✉ info@debutart.com
🌐 www.debutart.com

ilovedust is a small graphic design studio that specialises in creating innovative and unique design solutions. We specialise in brand creation and art direction and pride ourselves on being a complete solution to a host of creative briefs. Six parts English, one part Icelandic, one part Chinese and one part South African the studio pull influence and skill sets from a truly worldwide design playground. Different working styles and processes fuse together to produce award winning work worldwide. Previous clients incl: Nike, Coca-Cola, Shell, T Mobile, Intel, Sony, Red Bull F1 Racing, Renault, BBH, Publicis, Saatchi & Saatchi, J Lindberg, Samsung, Lucas Films, Levis and Hugo Boss, The BBC and Beyoncé. A full portfolio of ilovedust's work can be reviewed on-line at www.debutart.com

the coningsby gallery

Brand Jordan M4 for Nike.

Umbrella Girl Series. Personal piece.

Stills from PSA Animation for The Icelandic Department of Transport.

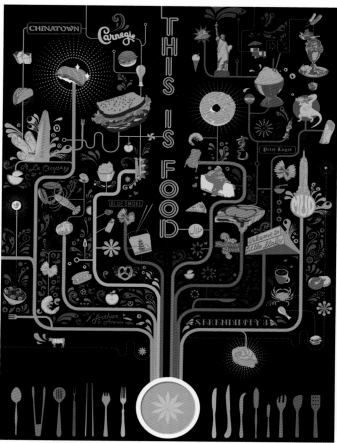

This Is Food for Visit New York City.

Umbrella Girl Series. Personal piece.

Collete for Spread Magazine.

Andrew Painter

15 Mornington Road
North Chingford
London E4 7DT
UK

T/F + 44 (0)20 8529 7469
M + 44 (0)7931 862 461
E candy@thepainters.me.uk
W www.contact-me.net/AndrewPainter

Cartoon Illustration
Character Design and Development
Designs for Flash
Cartoon Strip Art

Also see Contact 19–23.

Serge Seidlitz

Début Art & The Coningsby Gallery
30 Tottenham Street
London W1T 4RJ
UK

T + 44 (0)20 7636 1064
T + 44 (0)20 7636 7478
F + 44 (0)20 7580 7017
E info@debutart.com
W www.debutart.com

Serge Seidlitz lives and works
in London. He fuses his original
hand drawings with Mac software.
Serge worked for four years at
Cartoon Network/Toonami (Turner
Broadcasting) in print and on-air.

Previous clients incl: Shell, Vodafone,
Lucas Arts, BA, Bailey's, MTV, VH1,
Vodafone, KFC, The Cartoon Network,
Honda, Orange, Volvic, Nik Naks,

Reiker Shoes, The Times, The Guardian,
Top Gear Mag., Dazed & Confused,
Time Out, Mojo Mag., NME, BBC Music
Mag., John Brown Citrus Publishing,
Caspian Publ., Zip Design.

More of Serge's work can be found
in his extensive folio online at
www.debutart.com

'Hungerstrike'. Comm. by BBH Adv. for KFC.

'Tree'. Comm. by New Philanthropy Capital.

College Football cover image.
Comm. by the LA Times.

'Many Cultures, One World'. Comm. by BBH Adv.

British Airways January Sale. Comm. by BBH Adv.

Manchester International Festival. Comm. by Love Creative.

Women and Relationships. Comm. by Spin/Channel Four.

Robin Howlett

UK and Cyprus

T *+ 44 (0)203 002 0559*
T *+ 357 2563 4407*
E *illustration@howlett.eu.com*
W *www. howlett.eu.com*
W *www.contact-me.net/RobinHowlett*

Illustration for advertising, editorial, publishing and packaging.

Specialist in retro and art deco with over twenty years in the business. Versatile, adaptable, dependable – I won't let you down.

See my website for my cartoon and character design folio and Contact 23 for more examples.

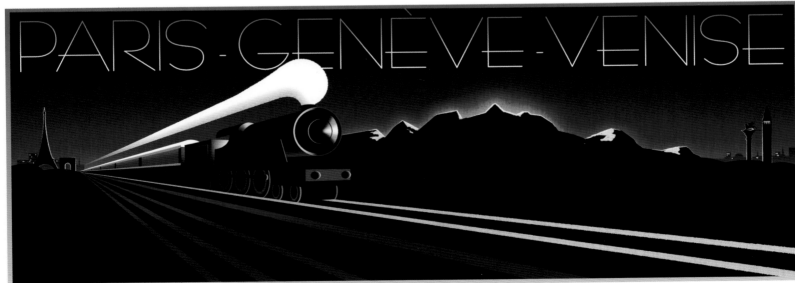

Sarah Kelly

Flat 2, 46 Osmond Road
Hove
East Sussex BN3 1TD
UK

T + 44 (0)1273 604 625
T + 44 (0)1273 735 915
M + 44 (0)7818 063 240
E sarahkelly@mistral.co.uk
W www.contact-me.net/SarahKelly
W www.the-annexe.com/sarah_kelly/page.html

See also Contacts 23, 20 and 18.

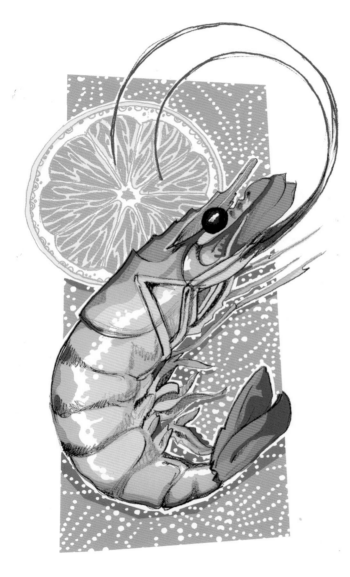

John Haslam

4 The Gates, Arthur Lane
Harwood
Bolton
Lancashire BL2 4JT
UK

T + 44 (0)1204 520 899
M + 44 (0)7950 301 222
E johnhaslam@popupencil.com
W www.contact-me.net/JohnHaslam

Piers Baker

4 Saxton
Parklands
Guildford
Surrey GU2 9JX
UK

☎ + 44 (0)1483 238 267
📱 + 44 (0)7889 128 331
✉ pbaker@piersbaker.co.uk
🌐 www.piersbaker.co.uk
🌐 www.contact-me.net/PiersBaker

Cartoons (inc. Vector artwork)
Children's Book Illustration
Syndicated Daily Strip Cartoonist
Packaging

Clients include Oxford University
Press, Pearson Education,
Cambridge University Press,
Thomson Nelson (Canada),
English Heritage, A&C Black,
Nelson Thornes, Letts, Unilever.

Visit www.cartoonslive.com
and learn about my 'live'
cartoon drawing displays.
Visit www.ollieandquentin.com
to see my daily cartoon strip
"Ollie and Quentin" about the
unlikely friendship between a
Seagull and a Lugworm. Distributed
by King Features Syndicate Inc.

Further samples in Contact 14 to 23.

Jacquie O'Neill

UK

☎ + 44 (0)1840 212 109
📱 + 44 (0)7971 010 730
✉ jacquie@jacquieoneill.com
🌐 www.jacquieoneill.com
🌐 www.contact-me.net/Jacquieoneill

Recent clients include: Adobe Systems Europe, Archant Life, BBC, Billington Cartmell, Cambridge University Press, Cedar Communications, Elle Girl, Emap Esprit, Fuji Hunt Europe, Future Publishing, Harper Collins, Highbury Entertainment Ltd, Hill & Knowlton, HQ Hair, IPC Media, Isis Publishing, Macmillan, National Rail Group, Oxford University Press, Pentacor Book Design, Vera Wang, Weetabix.

Matthew Cooper

Début Art & The Coningsby Gallery
30 Tottenham Street
London W1T 4RJ
UK

T + 44 (0)20 7636 1064
T + 44 (0)20 7636 7478
F + 44 (0)20 7580 7017
E info@debutart.com
W www.debutart.com

Matthew creates his unique illustrations with a strong graphic base, often featuring original photography and typographic elements.

Previous clients include: Franz Ferdinand/Domino, Deutsche Bank, The ENO, Logica, BA, TfL, The Royal Shakespeare Company, The British Council, The RMC Group, BP, Shell, BT, NASDAQ, RCA Records, The FT, The Sunday Telegraph, Time, New Scientist Mag., Campaign, Which? Mag, GQ Mag

Further examples of Matthew's work can be found in his extensive web folio at www.debutart.com

the coningsby gallery

Comm. By Future Publishing for a NetWeb Magazine article about on-line Travel Services.

Comm. by ASU for Carey School of Business (USA) Prospectus.

Comm. by M&C Saatchi for NatWest bank airport poster campaign.

Comm. by The Financial Times for an article about Wireless E-enabling.

Comm. by Financial World Magazine for article about off-shoring.

Chris Keegan

174 Ashley Gardens
Emery Hill Street
London SW1P 1PD
UK

T + 44 (0)7900 531 481
E ckeeganart@yahoo.co.uk
W www.chriskeegan.co.uk
W www.contact-me.net/ChrisKeegan

Maltings Partnership

Unit 32, The Derwent Business Centre
Clarke Street
Derby DE1 2BU
UK

T + 44 (0)1332 291 377
F + 44 (0)1332 346 928
E studio@maltingspartnership.com
W www.maltingspartnership.com
W www.contact-me.net/Maltings

The range of illustration styles that we can demonstrate continues to grow, with many clients turning to us because of our capacity to develop creative solutions reliably and efficiently. Be assured that all work is completed in-house and that our clients always liaise directly with the illustrator best suited to their requirements.

For further samples please refer to Contact 16 onwards, visit our website at www.maltingspartnership.com, or call Stephen Capsey, Michael Foster or Clive Baker on
T + 44 (0)1332 291 377

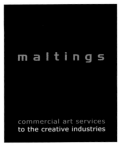

maltings

commercial art services
to the creative industries

Stephen Conlin

c/o Elfande Ltd
UK

☎ + 44 (0)1372 220 330
✉ info@pictu.co.uk
🌐 www.pictu.co.uk
🌐 www.contact-me.net/StephenConlin

Perspective, axonometric and isometric drawings, pictorial maps, location maps, coloured plans of buildings and cities. Archaeological and historical reconstruction drawings. Panoramic visualisations for development work.

Clients:
The Royal Household
English Heritage
Historic Scotland
The National Trust for Scotland
The National Trust
Country Life
Historic Royal Palaces
Grosvenor
Oxford University Press
St George's Chapel Windsor

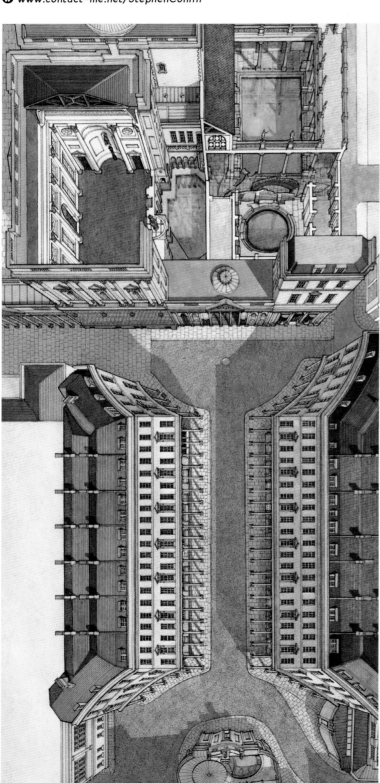

Bath

Lloyd's Building

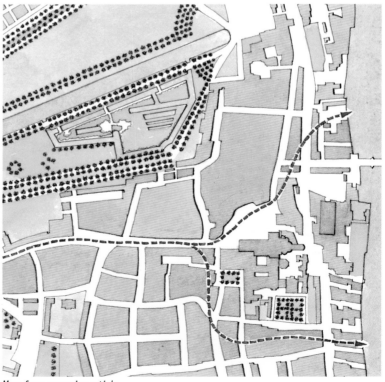

Map, for a magazine article

Susan Beresford

61 Tanfield Road
Croydon
Surrey CR0 1AN
UK

☎ + 44 (0)20 8686 9252
✉ info@susanberesford.co.uk
🌐 www.susanberesford.co.uk
🌐 www.contact-me.net/SusanBeresford

Colourful, painterly illustrations
in mixed media, and loose reportage
in pencil and ink.

Any subject.

All deadlines met.

Clients include: 4C, Beechcroft,
Bromley Education Development
Centre, Clarks International,
Clockwork, Caspian Publishing,
Croydon Council, Crystal Palace FC,
Heritage Lottery Fund, Minerva plc,
MQ Publications Ltd, Nestlé, One
World, Rafale Design, Schurman.

See also Contact 6–23.

Jerry Hoare

105 Kimberley Road
Penlayn
Cardiff CF23 5DP
UK

T *+ 44 (0)29 2049 8605*
E *jerry.hoare@ntlworld.com*
W *www.jerry-hoare.com*
W *www.contact-me.net/JerryHoare*

Chris Burke

17 Upper Grosvenor Road
Tunbridge Wells
Kent TN1 2DU
UK

☎ + 44 (0)1892 531 329
✉ christopher.burke@btclick.com
ⓦ www.chrisburke.org.uk
ⓦ www.contact-me.net/ChrisBurke

FT How To Spend It, The Times T2, BBC, Penguin Books, FT, Comic Relief, Time Magazine, GQ USA, Radio Times, Marks & Spencer, Punch, Tesco, Sony, Sunday Telegraph, Irish Tourist Board, Sunday Times, Guardian and almost every major British publication. Children's books wth Lenny Henry. TFL posters. Animation and theatre work. Over 80 murals for Ottakars bookshops.

Awards include Cartoonist of the Year and Creative Circle Gold Medal. Work in permanent collections of London Transport Museum and the V&A.

Work in all 24 Contacts.

Run for your life

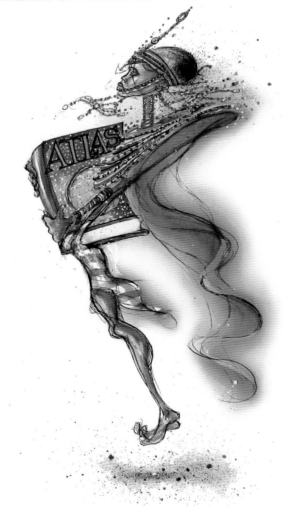

Waterstones/Ottakars Mural

Cameron Law

Flat 6
291 Leigham Court Road
London SW16 2RZ
UK

☎ + 44 (0)20 8769 3667
📱 + 44 (0)7950 433 922
✉ cam.law@virgin.net
🌐 www.contact-me.net/CameronLaw

Monster Illustration
🌐 www.monsters.co.uk

I am a long-standing member of
the Monster Illustration Group.

Clients (in no particular order)
include:

Guardian Newspaper Group
The Independent Newspaper

The Times Newspaper
FT Business Publications
Wardour Publishing
Centaur
Haymarket
Red Active Media Group
Reed Business Information
William Reed Publishing
Caspian Publishing
St Lukes
etc

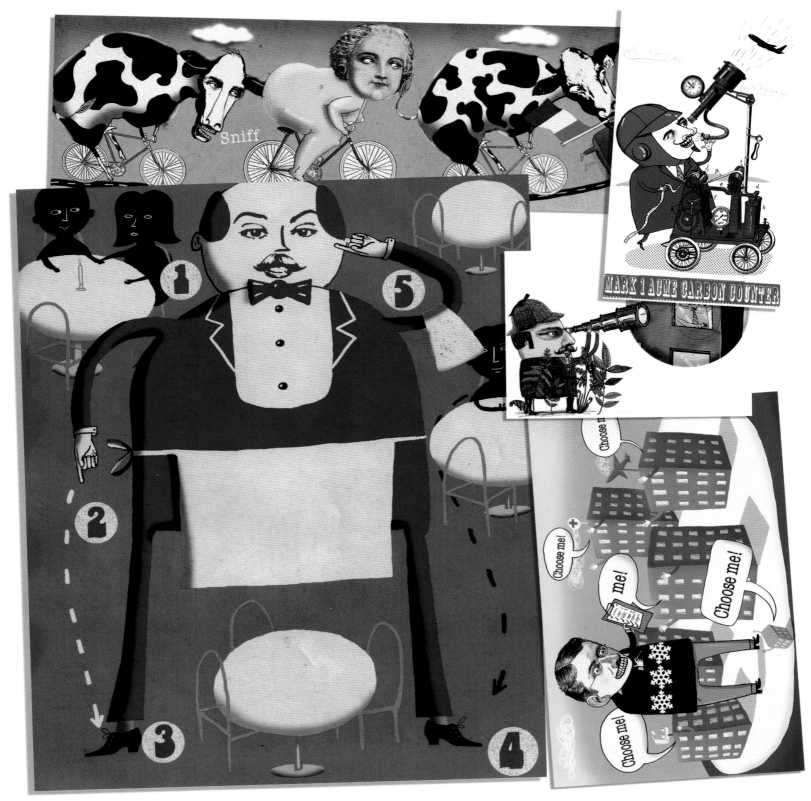

George Onions

UK

T + 44 (0)20 7193 2268
E alas@goatpix.com
W www.goatpix.com
W www.contact-me.net/GeorgeOnions

Decades of experience working for clients including Shell, Reckitt and Benckiser, Financial Times, Sesame, Yell, National Art Collection fund, Tate & Lyle, Observer, CAFOD, Braehead mall, Silverlink Trains and many more. Happy to generate ideas from the driest of copy or be guided by a thoughtful art director. Please see also web animation on my site.

Vanessa Wright

UK

☎ + 44 (0)2031 383 454
📠 + 44 (0)1908 216 683
📱 + 44 (0)7704 633 288
✉ vanessa@vanessawright.com
🌐 www.vanessawright.com
🌐 www.contact-me.net/VanessaWright

Experienced packaging illustrator specialising in impactful vector imagery for a wide range of UK and international clients such as

Dragon Brands, Jones Knowles Ritchie, Futurebrand, Brand Opus, Zigguratbrands, Taxi Studios, Barker Gray, Landor and Enterprise IG.

Eric Smith

124 Kennel Lane
Fetcham
Leatherhead
Surrey KT22 9PW
UK

T + 44 (0)1372 456 378
M + 44 (0)7747 126 831
E erics@zoom.co.uk
W www.ericsmith-art.co.uk
W www.contact-me.net/EricSmith

A greater variety of styles can be
viewed at ericsmithillustrator.co.uk

Clare Nicholas

16 Viaduct Close
Rugby
Warwickshire
CV21 3FD
UK

☎ + 44 (0)1788 543 276
Ⓜ + 44 (0)7711 274 918
Ⓔ clare.nic@btinternet.com
Ⓦ www.contact-me.net/ClareNicholas

Editorial, Advertising, Publishing
and Design.

Clients include:
Southampton University,
Reed Business Information, TUC,
British Association of Counseling
and Psychotherapy, Redwood Group,
RCN Publishing, Caspian Publishing,
Defra.

Gait Identification Study – Southampton University

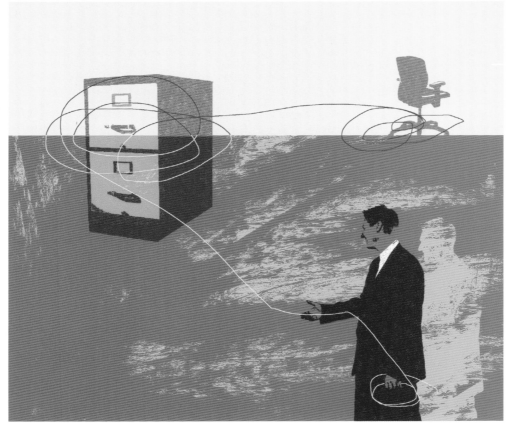

*Seizure of goods for rent arrears –
Reed Business Information*

Jovan Djordjevic

18 Elm Grove
Wivenhoe
Colchester
Essex CO7 9AY
UK

☎ + 44 (0)1206 822 118
📱 + 44 (0)7788 778 296
✉ jovan@jovan.demon.co.uk
🌐 www.jovandjordjevic.com
🌐 www.contact-me.net/JovanDjordjevic

Clients include:
BBC Worldwide, Centaur, Cover,
Dennis, Dorling Kindersley, Emap,
Euromoney, Finanzen, Findlay,
Fortune (USA), Future, Harrods,
Incisive Media, John Brown, Macmillan,
Martin Leach, Miller Freeman, MCC,
National Perry Motorpress, Playboy,
Prospect, Reader's Digest, Redwood,
Reed, Tolley, VNU, Wirtschaftswoche,
Wolf Ollins, Ziff Davies,

Sunday Business, Daily Telegraph,
Scotland on Sunday, Sunday Telegraph,
ES Magazine, Financial Times,
Guardian, Independent, Observer,
Time Out, Times Supplements, etc.

Also see Contact 12, 13, 14, 15, 16,
17, 18, 19, 20, 21, 22 & 23.

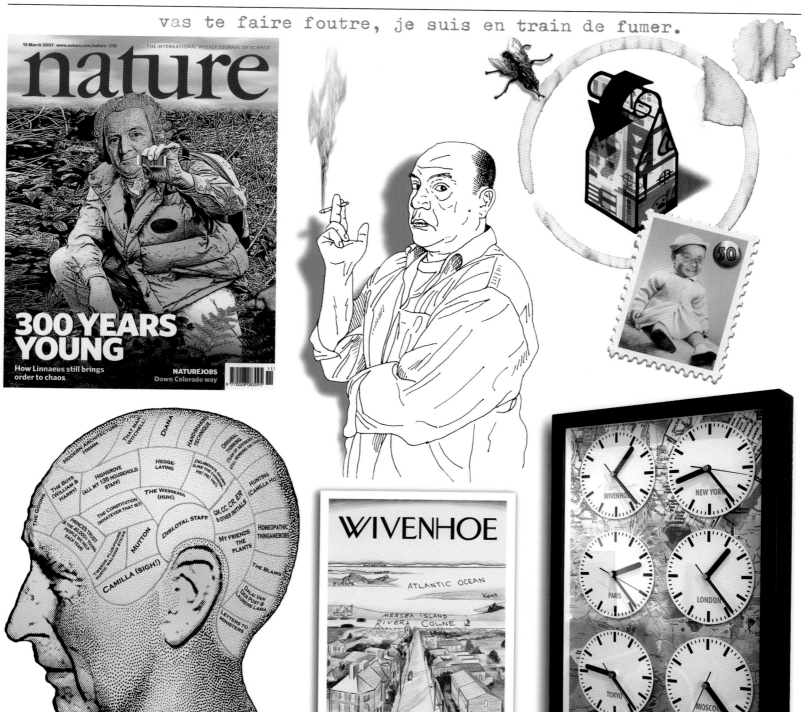

David Manktelow

East Sussex
UK

T + 44 (0)1892 770 141
M + 44 (0)7717 500 587
E david.manktelow@btconnect.com
W www.davidmanktelow.co.uk
W www.contact-me.net/DavidManktelow

I am a freelance illustrator based
in Hartfield, East Sussex. I work
traditionally and digitally creating
a wide variety of styles in many
media for storyboards, visuals,
artwork and websites, from simple
sketches through to finished art.

Ronald Wilson

29 Wooddale Green
Ballycullen View
Firhouse
Dubin 24
Ireland

T/F + 353 (0)1 493 5240
M + 353 (0)86 2386729
E info@ronwilsonillustration.com
W www.ronwilsonillustration.com
W www.contact-me.net/RonaldWilson

Vault49

Début Art & The Coningsby Gallery
30 Tottenham Street
London W1T 4RJ
UK

T + 44 (0)20 7636 1064
T + 44 (0)20 7636 7478
F + 44 (0)20 7580 7017
E info@debutart.com
W www.debutart.com

We design for our own pleasure first and foremost. We bring this personal passion and commitment to every brief. As long as there is room for inspiration and creativity we are as happy working on a CD cover for an independent artist as we are for an international media campaign.

Previous clients incl: Samsung, Coca-Cola, Nike, MTV, Levi's, Hed Kandi, Honda, Microsoft, LandRover, Intel, Greenpeace, VH1, Orange, Virgin, Chrysler, ITV, Channel 4, EMI, Nintendo, The New York Times, Wired Mag., Toni&Guy Mag.

More of Vault 49's work can be found in their extensive folio on-line at www.debutart.com

Comm. by Madame (Germany) for a Madame Magazine article about modern day interpretations of Greek mythology.

Comm. by Leo Burnett Adv. (Chicago) for a Samsung MP3 ad.

Comm. by Artful Dodger as a press ad for their apparel business.

Comm. by Rees Bradley Hepburn Adv. for LandRover POS and Direct Mail use.

Untitled. Self-initiated work.

Comm. by Latitude to advertise the QV shopping district in Melbourne (Australia).

Patrick Morgan

Début Art & The Coningsby Gallery
30 Tottenham Street
London W1T 4RJ
UK

T + 44 (0)20 7636 1064
T + 44 (0)20 7636 7478
F + 44 (0)20 7580 7017
E info@debutart.com
W www.debutart.com

Patrick's unique freehand style & approach has been attracting work from major brands worldwide for advertising, design, magazine editorial and book publishing. Patrick's predominantly freehand illustrations are all created on–system.

Previous clients incl:
Levi's, Virgin, MTV, Selfridge's, Nokia, Hewlett Packard, Siemens, Guinness,

Gordon's Gin, HMV, Toyota, The IOD, The Royal Academy, The British Library, The Body Shop, The ITE Group plc, Time Out, The Times, The Guardian, The Director Mag., Mojo, Creative Review, Q Mag., Community Care Mag.

More examples of Pat's work can be found in his extensive folio on–line at www.debutart.com

the coningsby gallery

Comm. by RBH for 'The Shires' retail complex.

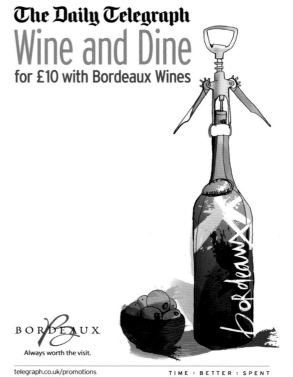

The Daily Telegraph
Wine and Dine
for £10 with Bordeaux Wines

BORDEAUX
Always worth the visit.

telegraph.co.uk/promotions

TIME : BETTER : SPENT

Comm. by The Daily Telegraph for Bordeaux Wines.

Comm. by BBH Adv. for GSK'S Niquitin anti-smoking product.

Waitrose
five a day
fresh ideas for summer

Comm. by Waitrose plc.

Damien Hirst. Comm. by The New York Times.

David Hockney. Comm. by The New York Times.

Comm. by The Independent on Sunday for their lifestyle section.

The London Eye. Comm. for British Airways.

James Taylor

Début Art & The Coningsby Gallery
30 Tottenham Street
London W1T 4RJ
UK

T + 44 (0)20 7636 1064
T + 44 (0)20 7636 7478
F + 44 (0)20 7580 7017
E info@debutart.com
W www.debutart.com

My illustration is adaptable. I draw, paint, scan, photograph, pull apart and put together (and not all in that particular order!). New technology offers me almost limitless possibilities but I find that it's my drawing skills, approach and keen graphic eye that really help. My head absorbs contemporary design and illustration, my feet are rooted in draughtmanship and tradition. Previous clients include: *Honda, Yahoo, Ernst & Young, Liberty's, Harrods, Nylon, MTV, Cream, VH1, SONY BMG, Time Out, NME, The New York Times, Esquire, Victionary, Carlos, Designersblock, The Observer, The Telegraph, The Independent, Strawberry Frog, Gas, Faber & Faber Books, Ninja Tunes. More of James' work can be found on pages 96–97 in Contact 23 and in his extensive folio online at www.debutart.com*

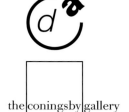

the coningsby gallery

'Hello It's Me'. Self-initiated piece.

Mumm-ra CD interior. Comm. by SONY BMG.

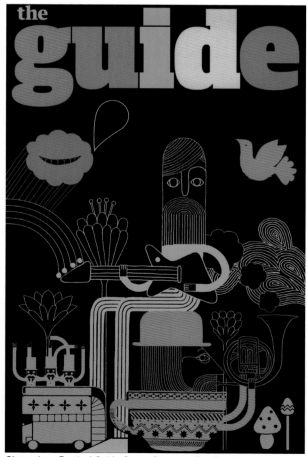

Glastonbury Festival Guide Cover. Comm. by The Guardian.

Comm. for Courtenay Marketing by Turnbull Ripley Design.

'Time To Get Rich'. Comm. for Brummel Mag. by Show Media.

'British Celebrities'. Comm. by Enroute Magazine.

Comm. by Firewood Comms (USA) for Louis Raphael apparel.

Hawaii

Début Art & The Coningsby Gallery
30 Tottenham Street
London W1T 4RJ
UK

☎ + 44 (0)20 7636 1064
☎ + 44 (0)20 7636 7478
📠 + 44 (0)20 7580 7017
✉ info@debutart.com
🌐 www.debutart.com

Hawaii was established in 2005 by Paul McAnelly. Based in London the studio offers a diverse range of skills including Design, Illustration and Art Direction. The studio prides itself on creating unique, original work from concept to print.

Previous clients incl: MTV, Liberty, Virgin Holidays, The British Film Festival, Universal Music, Land Rover, Matthew Williamson Fashion Design, Kew Gardens, GAP, Cartoon Network, Miss Selfridge, Redwood Magazine Publishing.

More of Hawaii's work can be found in his extensive folio on-line at www.debutart.com

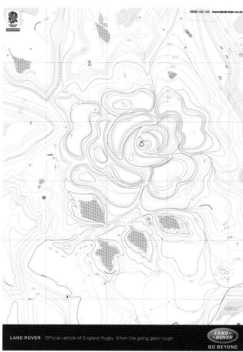

Comm. by RBH for Land Rover.

Self-initiated.

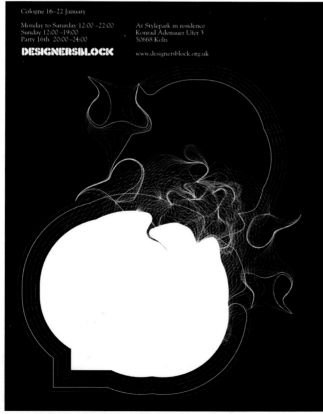

Comm. by Designersblock for their Cologne event.

Comm. by Liberty Store plc.

Comm. by Designersblock for their Milan event.

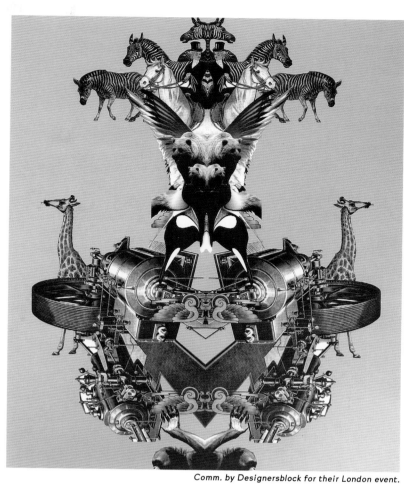

Comm. by Designersblock for their London event.

THE TIMES

BFI 51ST LONDON
FILM FESTIVAL
17 October – 1 November 2007

Comm. by The British Film Insitute for poster and press ads.

Designersblock
Frankfurt 06

At the invitation of
Messe Frankfurt
New product, lighting,
furniture from 30
international designers

Comm. by Designersblock for their Frankfurt event.

Matthew Dartford

Début Art & The Coningsby Gallery
30 Tottenham Street
London W1T 4RJ
UK

☎ + 44 (0)20 7636 1064
☎ + 44 (0)20 7636 7478
📠 + 44 (0)20 7580 7017
✉ info@debutart.com
🌐 www.debutart.com

Matt's unique approach and style to his digitally created images are attracting high profile clients worldwide in the advertising, design, editorial and entertainment sectors.

Previous clients incl:
The Ministry Of Sound, MTV, Cream Recordings, Virgin, American Express, Nestlé, Carlsberg, MacAfee, Schroders, Wrigleys, Flora, The Home Office/COI,

Monsoon Accessorize, Rolling Stone Mag., National Geographic Mag., The FT, Newsweek, New Scientist, Esquire, Digit Mag.

More examples of Matthew's work can be reviewed in his extensive portfolio on-line at www.debutart.com

the coningsby gallery

'Piggy Banks'.
Comm. by McMurray Publishing (USA).

'Building a Better World'. Comm. by Popular Science Magazine (USA).

'Godskitchen Electric'. Album cover comm. by ZIP Design for Godskitchen.

'Peperami'. Comm. for Unilever Foods by Billington Cartmell Adv.

'Cream Summer'. Comm. by ZIP Design for Cream Recordings.

Poster for WKD Vodka.

William Donohoe

30 Rugby Road
Brighton
East Sussex BN1 6EB
UK

☎ + 44 (0)1273 702 718
✉ mail@billdonohoe.com
W www.billdonohoe.com
W www.contact-me.net/WilliamDonohoe

28 years in illustration for design groups, advertising agencies, web designers and most major book publishers.

CD folio or printed package available on request.

For different subjects and styles see also: Contact books 12–23.

Tony Healey

Ground Floor, The Warwick Building
Kensington Village
Avonmore Road
London W14 8HQ
UK

T + 44 (0)20 7071 2334
F + 44 (0)20 7071 1056
M + 44 (0)7721 460 411
E tony.healey@stars.co.uk
W www.th-illustration.co.uk

Agent:
The Art Collection.co.uk

T + 44 (0)870 240 5001
F + 44 (0)870 240 5002
W www.artcollection.co.uk

Caricatures and Portraits

See also:
Contact 8–23 inclusive

David Banks

154 Maldon Road
Colchester
Essex CO3 3AY
UK

☎ + 44 (0)1206 520 792
📱 + 44 (0)7817 826 375
✉ david@bankscartoons.com
🌐 www.Bankscartoons.com
🌐 www.contact-me.net/DavidBanks

All my work can be supplied via email, disc or on the back of a beer mat.

Previous clients include: Arsenal FC, Battersea Dogs Home, Blockbuster Video, Chelsea FC, DC Thomson, Elsevier, Emap, Haymarket, IN2, Jane's Information Group, Manchester Utd FC, MAN Truck and Bus, Momentum Worldwide, Nestlé, Newcastle Utd FC, Pearson, RNLI, Sony, Schering, The Daily Mail, The Daily Telegraph, Vapet.

Please see previous Contacts for more samples.

Kathy Wyatt

Stableyard Studios
52 Egerton Road
Bishopston
Bristol BS7 8HL
UK

☎ + 44 (0)117 924 3929
📱 + 44 (0)7721 881 506
✉ kathy@kathywyatt.com
🌐 www.kathywyatt.com
🌐 www.contact-me.net/KathyWyatt

Recent clients include :

Oil of Olay/Saatchi, USA
Heaven Chocolates/JWT, London
Johnson & Johnson Babycare/Ideas, London
McClellands Whisky/Nevis Design, Scotland
Somerfield Wines/Vibrandt, London
Unplugged Play/Workman Publishing, USA

The Mini Story/Interone Publishing, China
The Guardian Newspaper
Woman & Home Magazine

Kathy Wyatt
www.kathywyatt.com

THE HENLEY COLLEGE LIBRARY

Mark Beech Illustrations Ltd

UK

T + 44 (0)20 7729 0916
M + 44 (0)7812 001 264
E mark_beech@btconnect.com
W www.nbillustration.co.uk (Agent)
W www.contact-me.net/MarkBeech

David Lyttleton

UK

☎ + 44 (0)1782 613 564
📱 + 44 (0)7958 421 092
✉ david.lyttleton@virgin.net
🌐 www.contact-me.net/DavidLyttleton

Clients have included:
The Guardian
Reader's Digest
The Times
The Daily Telegraph
Financial Times
Time Out
Sunday Tribune
The Scotsman
Sunday Express

Future
IPC
The Independent
BBC
John Brown
Building
EMAP
Penguin
and many, many more

Martin O'Neill

Début Art & The Coningsby Gallery
30 Tottenham Street
London W1T 4RJ
UK

T + 44 (0)20 7636 1064
T + 44 (0)20 7636 7478
F + 44 (0)20 7580 7017
E info@debutart.com
W www.debutart.com

Martin's work evolves from a fusion of collage, silkscreen, paint, transfers and photocopies. Fifteen years of experimental image making has resulted in his unique and instantly recognisable brand of illustration. Martin works for a wide range of international clients encompassing advertising, design, editorial and book publishing, as well as regular contributions to the UK and US press.

Recent clients incl: Guinness USA, Converse, Glenmorangie, Seeds of Change, Land Rover Freelander, BMW, The Folio Society, Historic Scotland, RSPB, UNICEF, GlaxoSmithKline, Crown Prosecution Service, The New York Times, The Boston Globe, The Chicago Tribune, The Guardian, The Sunday Telegraph. Further examples of Martin's work are in his extensive portfolio on-line at www.debutart.com

the coningsby gallery

Four of twenty six illustrations for Glenmorangie Single Malt Scotch Whisky. Commissioned by Story UK.

*SIC Recordings 12" Sleeve Illustration and Logo.
Comm. by Z Audio.*

Landrover Freelander. Comm. by TMW.

'Freedom of Speech'. Comm. By The Guardian Guide.

Edinburgh Fringe Festival Guide Cover. Comm. by Guardian Guides.

One of ten Illustrations for the book 'On Liberty'.
Comm. by The Folio Society.

25 Years of Arts at the Barbican. Comm. by The Sunday Observer.

James Carey

Début Art & The Coningsby Gallery
30 Tottenham Street
London W1T 4RJ
UK

☎ + 44 (0)20 7636 1064
☎ + 44 (0)20 7636 7478
📠 + 44 (0)20 7580 7017
✉ info@debutart.com
🌐 www.debutart.com

James' highly contemporary freehand line style and approach has been attracting assignment work from a wide variety of clients worldwide.

Previous clients include: Levi's, Adidas, Ted Baker, 55DSL, VH1, Harvey Nichols, Sony, Red Bull, Magners Cider, Carlos Magazine, Blueprint Mag., NME, Carhartt, Royal Elastics, The Observer, The Guardian, Esquire Magazine, Maxim Mag.

More of James' work can be reviewed on pages 110–111 in Contact 23 and in his extensive portfolio online at www.debutart.com

the coningsby gallery

ENJOY MAGNERS SENSIBLY

Comm. by Young Euro RSCG (Dublin) for Magners Cider ad campaign.

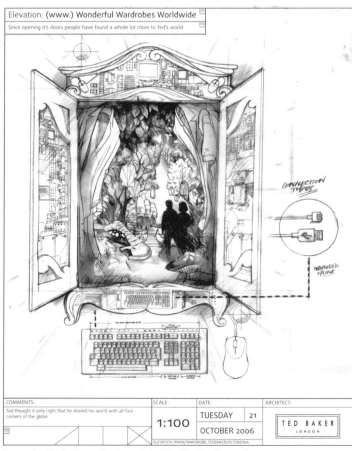

Comm. by No Ordinary Designer Label for The Ted Baker Co. Annual Report.

'Jean Reno'. Self-initiated piece.

Comm. by VW Driver Magazine.

Comm. by Cream Publishing for Carphone Warehouse.

BELIEVE
ADIDAS TECHFIT
ENGINEERED FOR THE IMPOSSIBLE

adidas.com/techfit

adidas
TECHFIT

Comm. by Iris for Adidas Techfit press and poster ad campaign.

Gabriella Buckingham

35 Happisburgh Road
North Walsham
Norfolk NR28 9HB
UK

☎ + 44 (0)1692 404 755
📱 + 44 (0)7984 164 926
✉ gabsbuckingham@gmail.com
🌐 www.contact-me.net/GabriellaBuckingham

I have been working as an illustrator since leaving art college in Kingston Upon Thames in the early 1990's.

My work spans children's books, greeting cards, gift wrap, editorial and more unusual one-off commissions.

Andy Baker

Début Art & The Coningsby Gallery
30 Tottenham Street
London W1T 4RJ
UK

☎ + 44 (0)20 7636 1064
☎ + 44 (0)20 7636 7478
📠 + 44 (0)20 7580 7017
✉ info@debutart.com
🌐 www.debutart.com

Andrew works with crisp colours and clean lines in pursuit of clear graphic communication. His illustrations are developed in Freehand, from pencil roughs. Final artwork can be e-mailed in any required format or sent on a CD or DVD.

Recent clients include: Toyota, Nokia, NatWest Bank, NASDAQ, Xansa, Abbey, The Harvard Business Review, The Henley Forecasting Centre, Time Warner Books, The New York Times, The Economist, Design Week, The Financial Times, New Scientist Mag., The Radio Times, John Brown Citrus Publ., idFX Mag., The Investor's Chronicle.

More examples of Andrew's work can be found in his extensive folio on-line at www.debutart.com

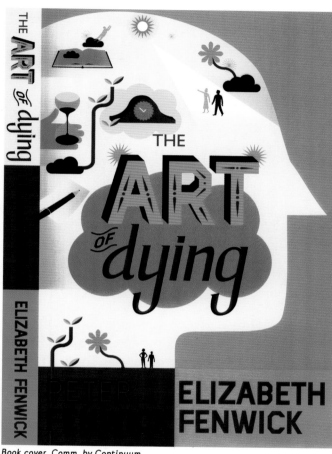

Book cover. Comm. by Continuum.

Comm. by The Director for article about self-centred managers.

Comm. by King's College London to promote TELOS a technology think tank in their University Report.

The Comic Stripper

Anthony Williams
1 Brandy Cove Road
Bishopston
Swansea SA3 3HB
UK

☏ + 44 (0)1792 230 047
✉ info@comicstripper.co.uk
✉ comicstripper@mac.com
ⓦ www.comicstripper.co.uk
ⓦ www.contact-me.net/TheComicStripper

Anthony Williams, The Comic Stripper.

The home of comic strips, illustration, storyboards, concept, style guide and licensed art.

We are also a custom comics publisher, able to take your idea from inception to publication.

Twenty years of very happy clients. Take a look at the website to find out why.

Lucy Truman

New Division
5 Risborough Street
London SE1 OHF
UK

T + 44 (0)20 7593 0505
F + 44 (0)20 7593 0501
E info@newdivision.com
W www.newdivision.com
W www.contact-me.net/LucyTruman

My clients list:

Avon, Braun, Garnier, Price Waterhouse Cooper, Paperchase, Penguin Books, Pentacor, OUP, Harper Collins, Transworld Publishing, Random House, American Girl, Pocket Books USA, Simon & Schuster USA, Hearst Media USA, Condé Nast USA, UK and Germany, Cosmopolitan NI,

Natmags UK, Delicious Magazine, Sainsbury's Magazine, You Magazine Mail on Sunday, Sunday Times, Sunday Express, Woman's Weekly and TV Times.

The Organisation

UK Office

📞 0845 054 8033 (UK only)
📞 + 44 (0)20 7833 8268
📠 + 44 (0)20 7833 8269
📱 + 44 (0)7973 172 902
✉ info@organisart.co.uk
🌐 www.organisart.co.uk
🌐 www.contact-me.net/TheOrganisation

New York Office

Pauline Mason

📞 + 1 917 586 6514
✉ masonpmac@yahoo.com

Over 70 portfolios online –
Cutting edge international image
makers.
Search by
Style – Medium – Subject Matter
Large Stock Library online –
Easy solutions to impossible deadlines
Purchase your favourite artwork –
www.illustrationgallery.co.uk

the organisation

Adrienne Salgado

Andres Martinez Ricci

Alex Steele-Morgan

0845 054 8033 www.organisart.co.uk info@organisart.co.uk

Angela Swan

David Dean

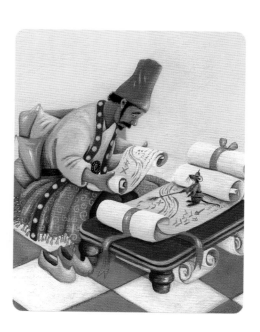

Carol Liddiment

0845 054 8033 www.organisart.co.uk info@organisart.co.uk

Annie Boberg

Bernice Lum

Martin Impey

The Tree House
41 Salisbury Road
Baldock
Herts SG7 5BZ
UK

T + 44 (0)1462 615 930
M + 44 (0)7810 543 676
E martin.impey@ntlworld.com
W www.martinimpey.com

Illustrations for children's books, magazine editorials, greeting cards and gifts, character development, story boards, games and puzzles etc.

Also in Contacts 10 to 23. Please contact me if you would like to see further examples or check out the website.

For licensing enquiries contact Emilie James at The Tree House on
T + 44 (0)1462 615 785
E emilie@thetreehousegallery.com
W www.thetreehousegallery.com

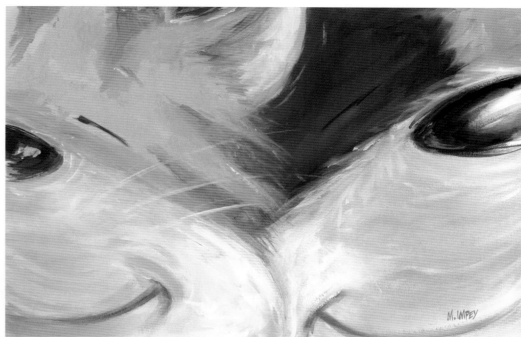

'FIRST CATCH OF THE DAY!'

Jane Smith

Courtyard Studio
38 Mount Pleasant
London WC1X OAP
UK

T + 44 (0)20 7833 4113
M + 44 (0)7905 350 383
E janeillustration@blueyonder.co.uk
W www.janeillustration.co.uk
W www.contact-me.net/JaneSmith
W www.theaoi.com/artist/janesmith

Any subject, any deadline.

Clients include:
The Guardian
The Times, The Daily Telegraph
The Times Educational Supplement
The Financial Times
City and Guilds
Harcourt Education
Oxford University Press
The Ivy Press, The Daily Express

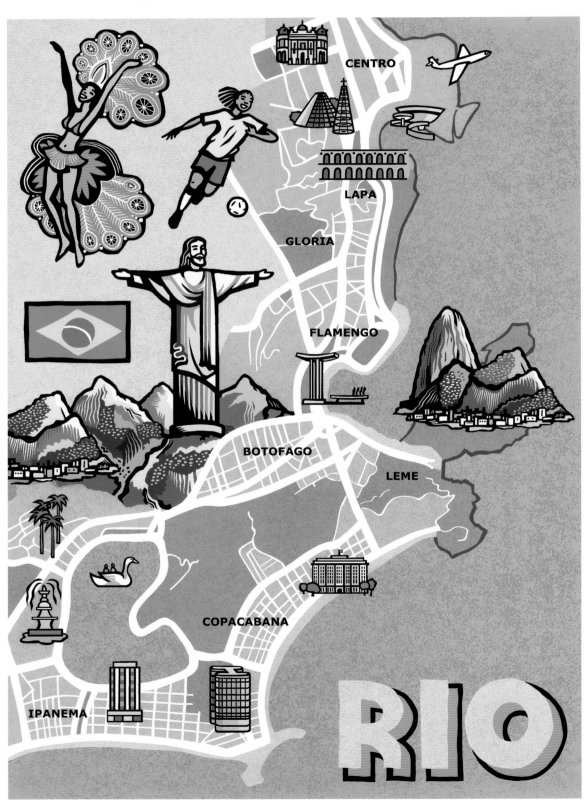

Vince McIndoe

Début Art & The Coningsby Gallery
30 Tottenham Street
London W1T 4RJ
UK

T + 44 (0)20 7636 1064
T + 44 (0)20 7636 7478
F + 44 (0)20 7580 7017
E info@debutart.com
W www.debutart.com

Vince's unique traditional painting and poster art styles attract clients worldwide. He has received numerous awards for his paintings and illustrations.

Previous clients incl: Coca-Cola, Singapore Airlines, Sony/CBS, Estée Lauder, Honda, American Express, BMW, Braun,

Molson Brewing Co., Kraft General Foods, Inter Continental Hotels, Nestlé, Reckitt/Coleman, Waterman Pens, Tetley Teas, Xerox, Time Mag., Wine Spectator Mag., Washingtonian Mag.

Further examples of Vince's work can be found in his extensive portfolio on the web at www.debutart.com

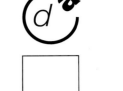

the coningsby gallery

Comm. for The Chesapeake Wine Festival.
Italian wine style poster.

Comm. by Showmedia for Stolichnaya Vodka poster.

Comm. for ColaPasta. Limited edition series of coffee posters.

Comm. by Seven Squared for a Fortnum & Mason ad
'The Art of Pampering'.

Beccy Blake

UK

☎ + 44 (0)1588 640 632
📱 + 44 (0)7810 170 542
✉ beccs@beccyblake.co.uk
🌐 www.beccyblake.co.uk
🌐 www.contact-me.net/BeccyBlake

Clients include:
BBC Worldwide, Egmont, Evans Brothers Ltd, Asda Magazine, Brown Publishing (USA), Brands2Life, Cambridge University Press, Franklin Watts (Hachette), Girlguiding UK, Harper Collins, Harcourt, Hodder Children's Books, HDRA (Garden Organic), Intervisual Books (USA),

John Brown Junior, John Lewis, Kamœ Design, Macmillan, The Hop Farm, Oxford University Press, Pearson, Puzzler Media, Scholastic (UK & USA), The Independent, Think Publishing, Times Educational, Waterlife Magazine, Wayland Books (Hachette), West Oxon District Council, ZSL London Zoo.

"Animal Tea Party"

Boy character sketches. Comm. by Oxford University Press

"Car full" Self Initiated

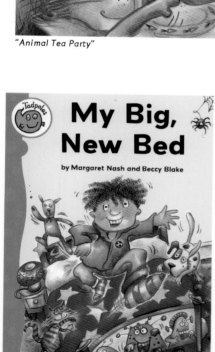

"My Big New Bed" Comm. by Franklin Watts

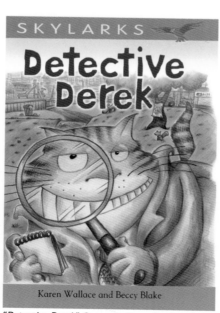

"Detective Derek" Comm. by Evans Brothers Ltd

"Shaun The Sheep" Comm. by Egmont

Chris Mitchell

Long Reach
Down Street
West Ashling
Chichester PO18 8DP
UK

📞 + 44 (0)1243 572 099
📱 + 44 (0)7802 874 349
✉ chris@chrismitchell.co.uk
🌐 www.epicicons.com
🌐 www.chrismitchell.co.uk

Chris Mitchell is recognised internationally for his unique skills in the development and exection of illustrative brand and corporate identity icons. Many have become global classics of our time. For a wider selection of his work please view Chris's online folio at: www.epicicons.com and back issues of this book, Contact. ©All rights reserved on images displayed. D&AD award winner.

Brand icon: Vinho Verde – Asda wines
Client: Elmwood. UK
Lettering design: Chris Weir

Corporate identity: John Dewar & Sons – Whisky
Client: EMG Communications. UK

Brand icon: BAFTA
Client: Rose. UK

Brand icon: Jordans – Foods
Client: BrandMe. UK

Brand icon: Maison Mau – Wine
Client: BrandMe. UK

GOLDEN HILL BREWERY
WIVELISCOMBE
EXMOOR ALES

Brand icon: Exmoor Ales – Beers
Client: CookChick Design. UK

Identity crest icon: Vatican Observatory
Client: Barker Gray. Australia

GLYNDE

Corporate identity: Clynde Place – Leisure
Client: Mosaic. UK

Iconic illustration: British Hotel Reservation Centre
Client: Bullet Design. UK

Brand icon: Sainsbury's – Foods
Client: Parker Williams. UK

www.epicicons.com

Chris Mitchell Tel: + 44 (0)1243 572 099

Nicola Streeten

Reading Room & Chapel
High Street
Wellingore
Lincoln LN5 0HW
UK

T + 44 (0)1522 811 809
M + 44 (0)7903 474 006
E info@nicolastreeten.com
W www.nicolastreeten.com
W www.contact-me.net/NicolaStreeten

See also:
Contact 21 p. 348
Contact 20 p. 133
Contact 23 p. 72

Sally Pinhey

664 Dorchester Road
Upwey
Dorset DT3 5LE
UK

☎ + 44 (0)1305 813 307
📱 + 44 (0)7719 923 434
✉ sallypinhey@tiscali.co.uk
🌐 www.sallypinhey.com
🌐 www.contact-me.net/SallyPinhey

Sally Pinhey, SGM, Mem AOI, is well-known in the botanical field and recipient of many RHS awards (see Contact 23). Illustrator of fruit books "Plums" and "Pears" by Jim Arbury, Fruit Superintendent at RHS Wisley.

Clients include Country Life, Church House Publications, Crabtree & Evelyn, Top That!, Aurum Press and Dorling Kindersley.

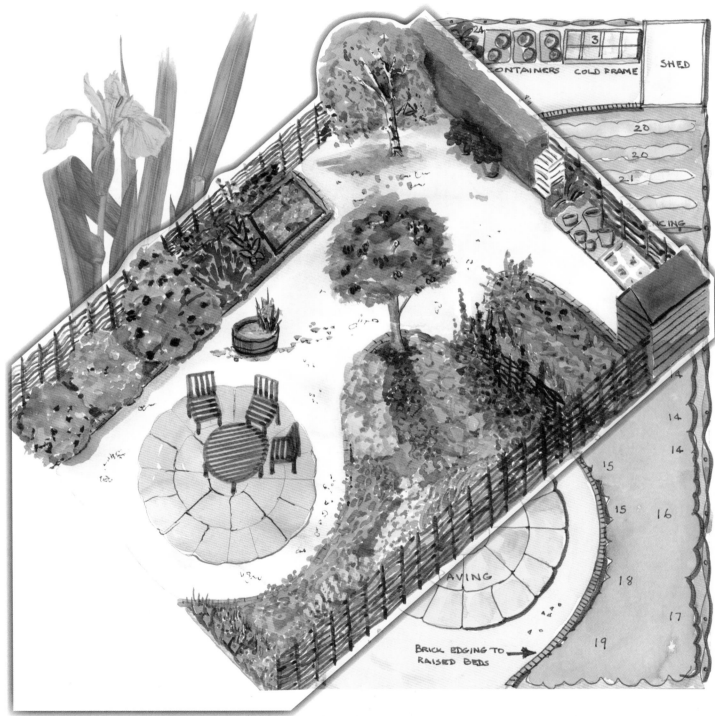

A Dyer's Garden; plan, axonometric projection of garden, and yellow flag iris for book "Dye Projects with Common Plants" by Judy Hardman

Nathan Daniels

Centrespace
6 Leonard Lane
Bristol BS1 1EA
UK

T + 44 (0)117 377 2337
M + 44 (0)7833 122 476
E *nathan@nathandaniels.com*
W *www.nathandaniels.com*
W *www.contact-me.net/NathanDaniels*

Distinctive, modern illustration.

Full, up to date portfolio and extensive client list at nathandaniels.com

Sophie Toulouse

Début Art & The Coningsby Gallery
30 Tottenham Street
London W1T 4RJ
UK

T + 44 (0)20 7636 1064
T + 44 (0)20 7636 7478
F + 44 (0)20 7580 7017
E info@debutart.com
W www.debutart.com

Sophie aims to create beautiful and powerful images with multiple layers to 'read'. A world where one's eyes and mind like to wander and dream (yes seriously!)

Previous clients incl:
Vodafone, Nike, IBM, Hugo Boss, Godiva, Honda, Smart, Nintendo, Céline, Chanel, Galeries Lafayette, Sony, Matador,

IFF (International Flavours and Fragrances), Veja, L'artisan Parfumeur, Lalique, Etam, Polydor. Magazine clients incl: Harper's Bazaar, Gloss, Flavor, Spray, Elle, Cosmopolitan, ArtTravel.

More of Sophie's work can be found in her extensive folio online at www.debutart.com

Wine packaging.

Personal piece. Nation of Angela (NOA).

Accessories. From a series of images commissioned by Muse Magazine (Italy).

One image from an Accessories series for Cream Magazine (Australia).

Comm. for Gloss Magazine.

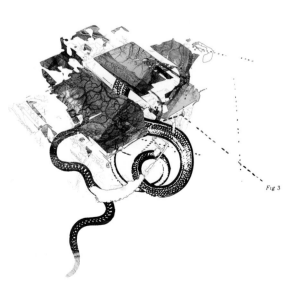

One image from an Accessories series for Cream Magazine (Australia).

Album cover image for Olivia Ruiz.

Alan McGowan

27 Waverley Place
Edinburgh EH7 5SA
UK

(M) + 44 (0)7980 845 629
(E) mail@alanmcgowan.com
(W) www.illustrationart.net
(W) www.contact-me.net/AlanMcGowan

I use mainly traditional materials (watercolour, ink, paint etc) to produce contemporary images.

Award winning projects have included a Clio for packaging, the Roses Advertising Awards Gold and Grand Prix winner, and D&AD Yellow Pencil Award for Be Books.

Clients include Marks and Spencer, Waitrose, National Trust for Scotland, Mercedes-Benz, Orion Books, Longmans, Countryfile Magazine, The Sunday Times, The Scotsman, The Independent, The Telegraph and many others.

Artwork can be supplied digitally, on transparency or as originals.

Saeko

Début Art & The Coningsby Gallery
30 Tottenham Street
London W1T 4RJ
UK

T + 44 (0)20 7636 1064
T + 44 (0)20 7636 7478
F + 44 (0)20 7580 7017
E info@debutart.com
W www.debutart.com

Saeko was born in Kyoto to a philosopher father and a painter mother. She moved to London in 1995 to study Illustration at Central St Martins College of Art & Design. Since graduation, she has been illustrating internationally on a wide variety of projects including packaging and fashion brand. Saeko uses watercolour, Photoshop & Illustrator. Saeko's artwork is strongly influenced by fashion and lifestyle and she loves challenging projects.
Previous clients incl: Sunday Times Style Mag., Waterstone's, Die Gestalten, Spirit & Destiny Mag., Trophy Life, Idea Design Mag., Gem Sportswear, Automobile Mag, Rapt Clothing.
More of Saeko's work can be found in her extensive portfolio on-line at www.debutart.com

the coningsby gallery

Comm. by 125 Magazine for their 'Touch' issue.

'Mermaid'. Image licensed to Rapt Clothing.

Personal piece.

Comm. by The Sunday Times' Style Magazine for an Agony Aunt column.

Andy Smith

UK

(M) + 44 (0)7949 997 978
(E) andy@asmithillustration.com
(W) www.asmithillustration.com
(W) www.contact-me.net/AndySmith

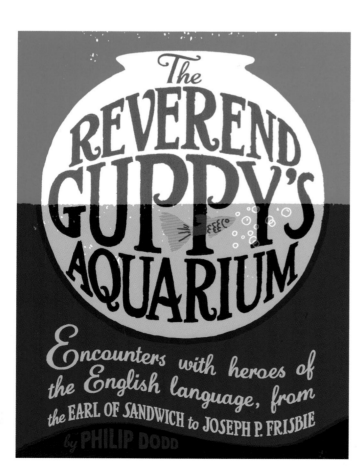

Deborah MacQueen

Aydon Hurst
Adon Road
Corbridge
Northumberland NE45 5EH
UK

T *+ 44 (0)1434 634 538*
M *+ 44 (0)7972 566 330*
E *info@deborahmacqueen.co.uk*
W *www.deborahmacqueen.co.uk*
W *www.contact-me.net/DeborahMacQueen*

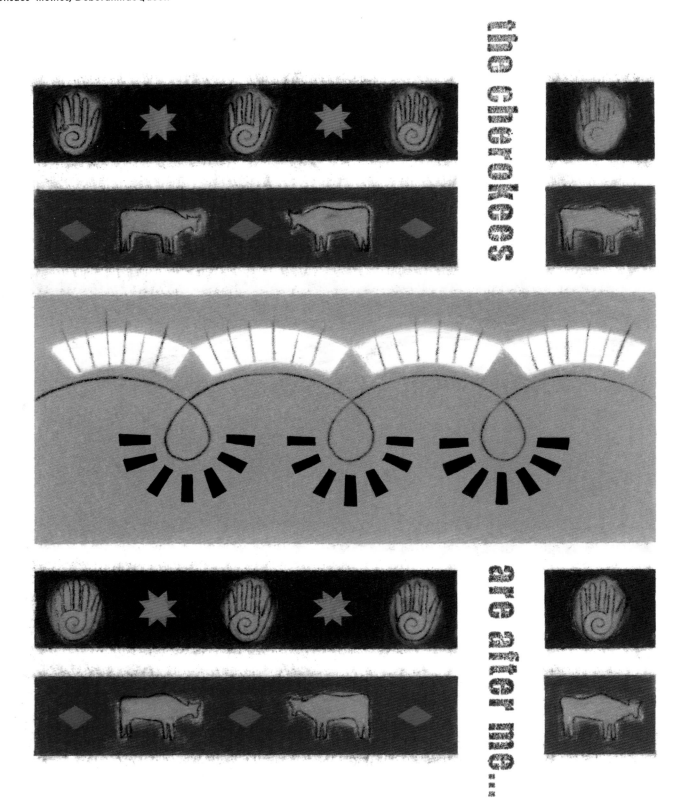

the cherokees are after me...

Deborah MacQueen

T + 44 (0)1434 634 538

Stephen Elford

Brighton
UK

☏ + 44 (0)7808 293 756
✉ studio@stephenelford.com
🌐 www.stephenelford.com
🌐 www.contact-me.net/StephenElford

Sally Newton

Brighton
UK

☎ + 44 (0)7734 544 108
✉ contact@sallynewton.co.uk
🌐 www.sallynewton.co.uk
🌐 www.contact-me.net/SallyNewton

Established illustrator.
Images are created digitally using
vectors and scanned textures.

A style and method suitable for briefs
from all sectors.

Recent clients have included
WHSmiths, Tesco and IPC Media.

Sarah Jones

Début Art & The Coningsby Gallery
30 Tottenham Street
London W1T 4RJ
UK

☎ + 44 (0)20 7636 1064
☎ + 44 (0)20 7636 7478
📠 + 44 (0)20 7580 7017
✉ info@debutart.com
🌐 www.debutart.com

Sarah's illustrations are a combination of on-system work, printmaking and photography. Sarah enjoys (and is excellent at) interpreting a brief and generating ideas. She is highly versatile and succesfully tackles a wide range of subjects.

Previous clients incl: HSBC, BP, Xerox, BA, The John Lewis Partnership, The British Medical Assoc., Decca Music, Abbey, The Royal Bank of Scotland, Marks & Spencer, Oxford University Press, New Scientist Mag., Moneywise Mag., Personnel Today Mag., Saga Mag., Voyager Mag., The Banker Mag.

More examples of Sarah's work can be found in her extensive folio on the web at www.debutart.com

the coningsby gallery

Commissioned by The Economist for an Economist Intelligence Unit Report on Pensions.

Self-initiated pieces.

Maria Taylor

32 Braemar Road
Nottingham NG6 9HN
UK

T + 44 (0)1159 172 124
M + 44 (0)7947 171 318
W www.contact-me.net/MariaTaylor

Previous clients include web images for the home office, Royal Bank of Scotland and business websites including Womengetsmart. Media Week Magazine, Haymarket Publishing, Murky Depths Comics, Toynbee Editorial, Shape Fitness, Join The Pink Parry Viral Campaign, Torchbox Ltd, sold designs to the greetings industry in America, ingenius exhibition work.

Work both traditionally and digitally in regards to work.

Yummy Mummy Culture

Carol del Angel

Début Art & The Coningsby Gallery
30 Tottenham Street
London W1T 4RJ
UK

T + 44 (0)20 7636 1064
T + 44 (0)20 7636 7478
F + 44 (0)20 7580 7017
E info@debutart.com
W www.debutart.com

Carol's freehand work combined with her unique on-system photo-collage style is attracting leading clients worldwide.

Previous clients incl: Orange, Honda, Barclaycard, TfL, Lexus Cars, EMI, Random House Books (USA), Little, Brown Books (USA), Target Stores (USA),TimeWarner Books, The Times, Time Out, Elle, Marie Claire, Cosmopolitan (USA), T3 Mag., Men's Health Mag., New Woman Mag., Fabric Mag., Computer Arts Magazine.

More of Carol's work can be found in her extensive folio on-line at www.debutart.com

Self-initiated.

Self-initiated.

Comm. by Marie-Claire Magazine for an article about women and men's feelings and experiences of monogamous relationships.

Satoshi Kambayashi

Flat 2
40 Tisbury Road
Hove
East Sussex BN3 3BA
UK

☏ + 44 (0)1273 771 539
📱 + 44 (0)7739 179 107
✉ satoshi.k@virgin.net
🌐 www.satillus.com
🌐 www.contact-me.net/SatoshiKambayashi

More works on view at
www.satillus.com

Clients include: The Economist,
The Guardian, New Statesman,
Abercrombie & Kent, Delicious,
Neue Zürcher Zeitung, PLC Magazine,
Land's End USA, Courrier Japon,
Fire Brigades Union, etc.

SATOSHI
ILLUSTRATION

The Art Market

UK

☎ + 44 (0)20 7407 8111
✉ info@artmarketillustration.com
🌐 www.artmarketillustration.com

THE ART MARKET
illustration agency

GRAHAM HUMPHREYS

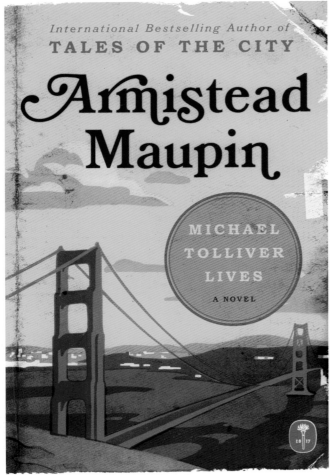

A new view of London

West End from Primrose Hill by Paul Catherall

Copies of this poster are available from London Transport Museum, Covent Garden Piazza.
© Transport for London 2007

MAYOR OF LONDON   Transport for London OVERGROUND

PAUL CATHERALL

SAMARA BRYAN

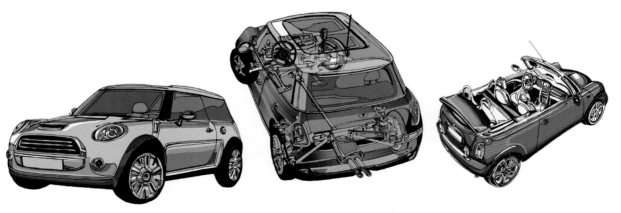

LUCY OLDFIELD

t +44 (0)20 7407 8111 e info@artmarketillustration.com www.artmarketillustration.com

RICHARD LEVESLEY

t +44 (0)20 7407 8111 e info@artmarketillustration.com www.artmarketillustration.com

DAVID MCCONOCHIE

t +44 (0)20 7407 8111 e info@artmarketillustration.com www.artmarketillustration.com

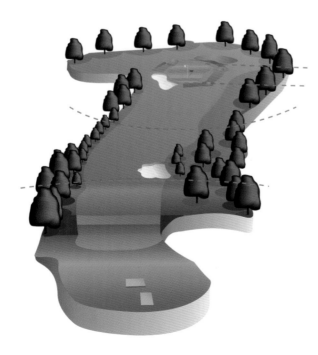

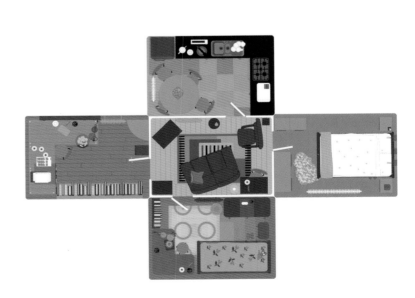

ANNE CAKEBREAD

t +44 (0)20 7407 8111 e info@artmarketillustration.com www.artmarketillustration.com

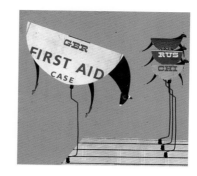

BEN HAWKES

PER KARLEN

t +44 (0)20 7407 8111 e info@artmarketillustration.com www.artmarketillustration.com

PER KARLEN

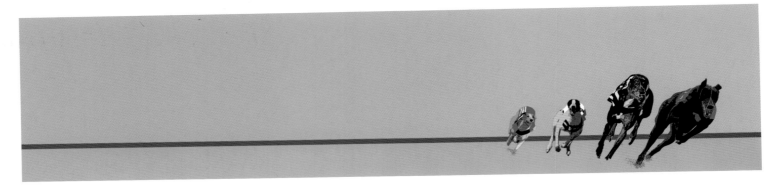

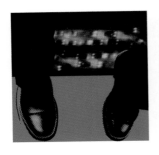

ANTHONY PIKE

t +44 (0)20 7407 8111 e info@artmarketillustration.com www.artmarketillustration.com

MIND THE
GAP!
· between expectation and reality

TURBO - 5000

TOM FROST

Sam McCullen

UK

M + 44 (0)7891 905 712
E info@sammccullen.com
W www.sammccullen.com
W www.contact-me.net/SamMcCullen

Agent:
Penny Holroyde
Caroline Sheldon Literary Agency
70–75 Cowcross Street
London EC1M 6EJ
UK

T + 44 (0)20 7336 6550
E pennyholroyde@carolinesheldon.co.uk
W www.carolinesheldon.co.uk

Clients include:
Leo Burnett,
Inferno,
BBC,
HIT Entertainment,
Hodder Children's Books,
HarperCollins Publishers,
Campbell Books,
Oxford University Press,
The Milk Development Council,
The School Milk Project.

Kevin O'Keefe

Début Art & The Coningsby Gallery
30 Tottenham Street
London W1T 4RJ
UK

T + 44 (0)20 7636 1064
T + 44 (0)20 7636 7478
F + 44 (0)20 7580 7017
E info@debutart.com
W www.debutart.com

Kevin sets out to make drawings that are very graphic and carefully designed. He has always had a fondness for the 'ligne claire' style of drawing and he is often referential to his heroes, from the Belgian comics to the US graphic novels, from Swaarte to Seth. He enjoys wit and a touch of the sinister, and intelligent use of colour if the job allows for this.

Previous clients incl: Air France, Heineken, Philips, Guinness, Adidas, Ford, Disney, British Gas, The Post Office, Punch, Time Out, The Radio Times, Melody Maker, Building Magazine, The Sunday Telegraph, Red Magazine, Time Magazine, The Listener.
More examples of Kevin's work can be found online in his folio on the web at www.debutart.com

the coningsby gallery

Studio Liddell Ltd

London & Manchester
UK

☎ + 44 (0)161 834 5150 (Manchester)
📠 + 44 (0)20 7269 8695 (London)
✉ Contact@studioliddell.com
🌐 www.studioliddell.com
🌐 www.contact-me.net/StudioLiddell

Digital Illustration, animation and design for advertising, TV, web, packaging and interactive media.

Please visit our comprehensive website for more examples & case studies.

ROARY
The Racing Car

www.studioliddell.com

Sarah Howell

Début Art & The Coningsby Gallery
30 Tottenham Street
London W1T 4RJ
UK

☎ + 44 (0)20 7636 1064
☎ + 44 (0)20 7636 7478
🖷 + 44 (0)20 7580 7017
✉ info@debutart.com
🌐 www.debutart.com

Sarah's unique photo-illustrative style & approach has been attracting clients worldwide for high profile advertising, design, magazine editorial & entertainment sector clients. Sarah's images all include freehand illustrative work. Sarah is both a photographer & illustrator, combining the two. Sarah can also work with supplied photography. Previous clients incl: NIKE, Coca-Cola, Nokia, Vodafone, EMI, Island Records, Universal Records, VH1, MTV, Illy Coffee, Harrods, Siemens, Jameson Irish Whiskey, Hewlett Packard, Proctor & Gamble (USA), Penguin Books, Luella Bartley, The Grammy's, Flaunt Mag., Madame V, Tank Mag., Maxim Mag., The Sunday Times, Time Out. More of Sarah's work can be reviewed on p184–185 in Contact 23 and in her extensive portfolio on-line at www.debutart.com

the coningsby gallery

'Growler'. Personal work for Illustrate: Designersblock exhibition.

Comm. by Digital Arts Magazine 2006 for feature about photography in illustration.

Comm. by BBH for Vodafone press and poster campaign.

Comm. by The Market Store for Vodafone below the line campaign.

Comm. by Celf Creative for The Welsh Assembly.

Comm. by Publicis Blueprint for Mal Life Magazine cover featuring Kitty Klaw (Burlesque artist).

'Bearded Lady'. Personal work for Illustrate: Designersblock exhibition.

Tim Ellis

Début Art & The Coningsby Gallery
30 Tottenham Street
London W1T 4RJ
UK

T + 44 (0)20 7636 1064
T + 44 (0)20 7636 7478
F + 44 (0)20 7580 7017
E info@debutart.com
W www.debutart.com

Tim's intelligent, concept-driven illustrations attract a broad range of clients across editorial, design, and advertising. He enjoys working both on open-ideas and specific briefs.

Previous clients incl:
Virgin Atlantic, Honda, BT, Talk Talk, Vodafone, The Samaritans, The BBC, The MOD, Microsoft, Reuters, RATP Metro (France), Mishcon de Reya,

Lloyds Bank, Brodies, Dsci4 Records, The RNID, The Times, The Guardian, The FT, The Economist, New Scientist, Director Mag., The Banker, The Big Issue, YOU Mag., Caspian Publ.

Further examples of Tim's work can be found in past Contact editions and in his extensive folio on the web at www.debutart.com

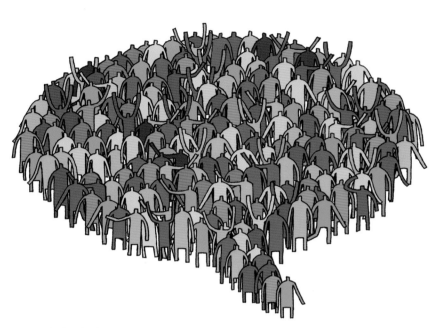

Comm. by Inside Housing for an article about community voice.

Comm. by Nokia for an internal Report.

Comm. by Edge Magazine for an article about fast food pharmacies.

Comm. by Mishcon de Reya for an article about share value inflation.

Comm. by Siemens for an article about Think Customer scheme.

Comm. by Mishcon de Reya for a poster about advice accuracy.

Comm. by Mishcon de Reya for a poster about advising clients at their level.

Brian Gallagher

Illustration
Dublin
Ireland

☎ + 353 (0)1497 3389
☎ + 353 (0)86 079 7200
✉ brian@bdgart.com
🌐 www.bdgart.com
🌐 www.contact-me.net/BrianGallagher

Leo Burnett Associates
Ogilvy & Mather
Scholz and Friends
Random House
Penguin
Longmans
Harper Collins
Reed Publishing
Orbis
Evening Standard
Le Monde

Gramophone
Sunday Independent
Observer
Sunday World
FHM
Economist
Trailfinders
Haymarket Group
Bar Review
e-three Bionic Creative
Eaglemoss

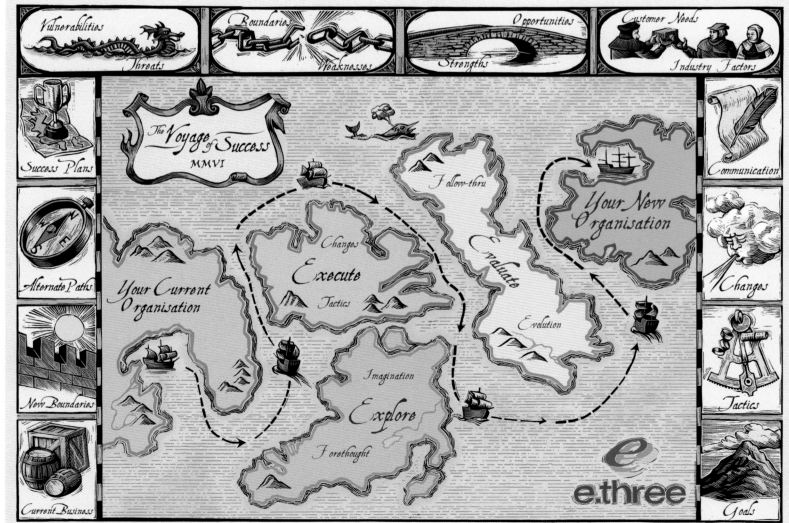

Ali Pellatt

Sydney
Australia

☎ + 61 (0)405 593 123
✉ ali@alipellatt.com
🌐 www.alipellatt.com
🌐 http://illustrationaustralia.blogspot.com
🌐 www.contact-me.net/AliPellatt
See website for landline

Recent clients: Proximity London, Heavenly Group, BT Vision, Wrigley's USA, TES, Seven Squared, Elvis Communications, Delicious, DK, Transworld, Public Finance Magazine, Sydney's Child, Reader's Digest, Centaur Publishing, Haymarket, Marmaladya.com

See Contact 16-23 for previous work and client lists.

BT Vision

Times Educational Supplement

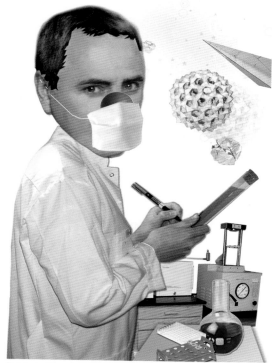

Reader's Digest

Dorling Kindersley 'Secrets' book

Kate Miller

UK

☎ + 44 (0)131 332 1883
📱 + 44 (0)7958 998 078
✉ kate@kate-miller.com
🌐 www.kate-miller.com
🌐 www.contact-me.net/KateMiller

Recent clients include:
Bloomsbury Publishing,
Barclays Bank, Daily Mail,
The Independent, The Cabinet Office,
The Guardian, Pizza Express,
Standard Life, The Financial Times,
Nickelodeon, The Original Tour
Company, Clarks Shoes,
Harper Collins Publishers.

To see further examples of my work,
please see previous editions of
Contact, or on my website.

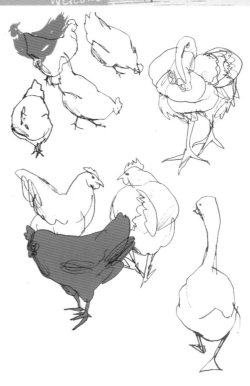

Peter Quinnell

Début Art & The Coningsby Gallery
30 Tottenham Street
London W1T 4RJ
UK

☎ + 44 (0)20 7636 1064
☎ + 44 (0)20 7636 7478
📠 + 44 (0)20 7580 7017
✉ info@debutart.com
🌐 www.debutart.com

Peter's unique collage, photo-collage and assemblage artworks, allied with his inimitable style and approach, attract clients worldwide for advertising, design, magazine, book and entertainment assignments.

Previous clients incl:
HMV, VCCP/LBC News Radio, Harvey Nichols (main window displays), Paul Smith, Channel 4,

Trouble TV, Headron/Cadbury–Schweppes, Tesco, Sainsbury's, The Team/3M, Point Blank/Trojan Records, The Independent, The Times Sunday Review, Random House Books, Penguin Books, Radio Times, The Mail on Sunday, GQ Mag., Esquire Mag.

Extensive portfolio free to view at www.debutart.com

the coningsby gallery

Comm. by And Partners for The Bluewater Shopping Centre.

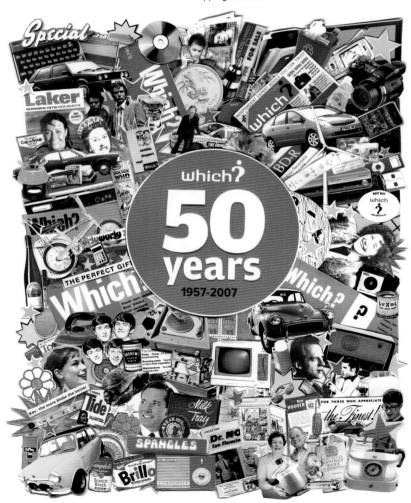

Comm. by WHICH? for WHICH? Magazine front cover.

Comm. by GQ Magazine.

Comm. by River Publishing.

Simon Roulstone

90 Woodlands Avenue
Eastcote
Ruislip
Middlesex HA4 9RH
UK

T + 44 (0)20 8868 2583
M + 44 (0)7941 411 908
E simon@roulstone.demon.co.uk
W www.roulstone.demon.co.uk
W www.contact-me.net/SimonRoulstone

See also Contact Illustrators 18 to 23.

Simon Roulstone
digital illustration

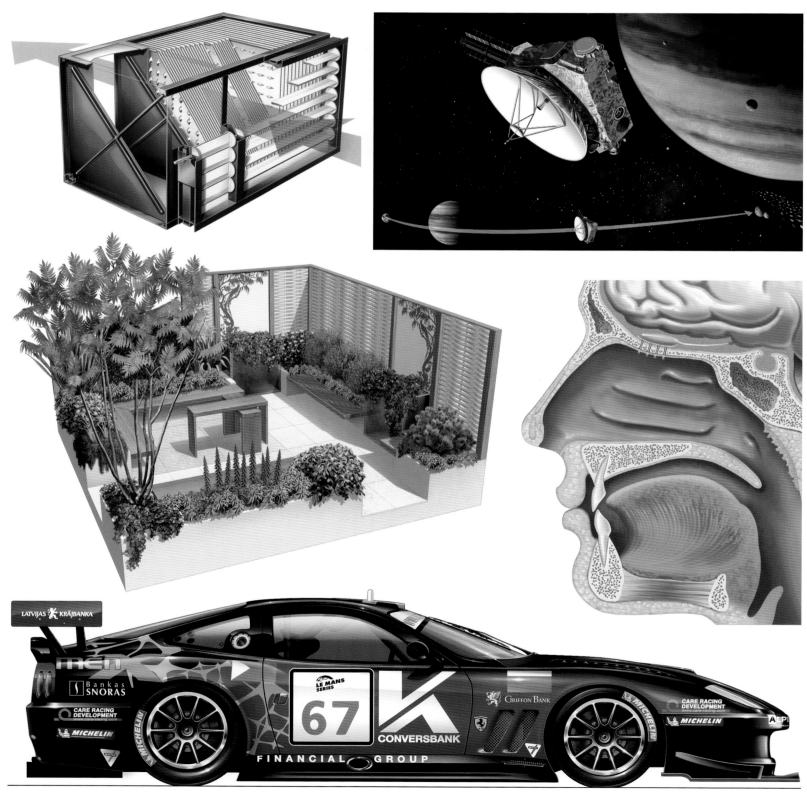

Kath Walker Illustration

Kath Hextall
Greydene, 13 Boys Lane
Fulwood
Preston PR2 3QX
UK

T/F + 44 (0)1772 712 154
M + 44 (0)7835 255 053
E info@kathwalker-illustration.co.uk
W www.kathwalker-illustration.co.uk
W www.contact-me.net/KathWalker

See also Contacts 10–23.

Robyn Neild

UK

📞 + 44 (0)7855 344 239
✉ Robyn@RobynNeild.com
🌐 www.RobynNeild.com

Clients include:

Vogue, Harpers & Queen, Elle,
Tatler, Glamour, Red Magazine,
The Daily Telegraph, The Guardian,
Patrick Cox, Victoria's Secret,
Givenchy, Vivienne Westwood,
Stephen Jones, Hardy Amis, MaxMara,
Revlon, Marks & Spencer,

United Airlines, Nails Inc,
Charles Worthington, Thomas Pink,
Orion books, HarperCollins,
Random House, Penguin Books,
Harrods, Harvey Nichols,
Dickins & Jones, Liberty.

See also:
Contact 17, 18, 19, 20, 21 & 22

Mathew Hall

3 James Terrace
Church Path
Mortlake SW14 8HB
UK

☎ + 44 (0)20 8876 0580
📱 + 44 (0)7973 761 196
✉ mat@mathewhall.co.uk
🌐 www.mathewhall.co.uk
🌐 www.contact-me.net/MathewHall

I have been illustrating and visualisng for 13 years and have produced my work on computer for the last 8 years, so I am able to combine traditional skills and experience with the latest digital techniques. As each client has such specific requirements, I have developed a broad range of styles from photo-realistic to soft painterly to graphic icons. If you would like see more of my work please visit my website or email me for samples. Clients include: Beechams, Benilyn, Camel, Coca-Cola, Douwe Egberts, Famous Grouse, Head & Shoulders, Homebase, J2O, John Smith's, Knorr, Lyles, Marks & Spencer, Mars, Nintendo, Persil, Walkers Crisps, Twinings of London, Waitrose, Whittard of Chelsea.
See also Contact 19 page 58 and Contact 23 page 100.

Camel

Spar

Neil Webb

Début Art & The Coningsby Gallery
30 Tottenham Street
London W1T 4RJ
UK

☎ + 44 (0)20 7636 1064
☎ + 44 (0)20 7636 7478
📠 + 44 (0)20 7580 7017
✉ info@debutart.com
🌐 www.debutart.com

Neil's illustration style and approaches are attracting clients across the advertising, design, magazine editorial and book publishing industries.

Previous clients incl: The New York Stock Exchange, LaSalle Bank, British Airways, Verizon, Virgin Atlantic, SONY, The BBC, Royal Bank of Scotland, Buxtons Mineral Water, Strepsils, The Sunday Times, The Washington Post, The FT, The Economist, The Telegraph, The Guardian, The Independent, Bloomsbury Book Publ., New Scientist, Time Out, Design Week.

More examples of Neil's work can be found on pages 80–81 in Contact 23 and in his extensive and downloadable portfolio online at www.debutart.com

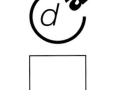

the coningsby gallery

Comm. by RCKR/Y&R for a Virgin Atlantic ad.

Self-initiated piece for cover of book 'The Iron Giant' by Ted Hughes.

Comm. by Fallon (USA) for a New York Stock Exchange ad 'Companies Flourish Here'.

Comm. by The Telegraph for a Rioja Wine promotion.

Comm. by Ode Mag. (USA) for an article about 'Democratic Capitalism'.

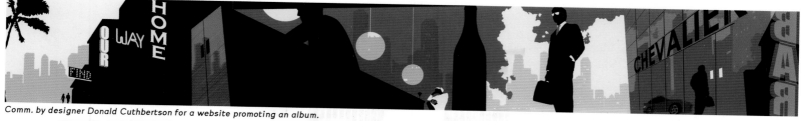

Comm. by designer Donald Cuthbertson for a website promoting an album.

Comm. by Oxford University Press for an article 'Chinese Whispers'.

Comm. by Surgery Creations for cover of Connect Magazine.
Feature: Services for Union members.

Comm. by The Observer for an article about online communities.

Pablo Bernasconi

Début Art & The Coningsby Gallery
30 Tottenham Street
London W1T 4RJ
UK

T + 44 (0)20 7636 1064
T + 44 (0)20 7636 7478
F + 44 (0)20 7580 7017
E info@debutart.com
W www.debutart.com

Pablo Bernasconi is an illustrator, graphic designer and writer. Pablo works with real objects making collages with volume. He changes the meaning of each element by mixing it with others. He works in mixed media, creating characters, portraits, scenes, etc. Previous clients incl: The Times, The New York Times, The Wall Street Journal, Rolling Stone Mag., Random House Books, Oxford University Press, The BBC, MTV, FOX Channel, New Scientist, J Walter Thompson Adv., Saatchi Adv., Shell, Nokia, Movistar, Renault, Houghton Mifflin Books, C&A, Clarin, La Voz de Galicia (Spain), La Nación de Costa Rica, Eureka! Magazine, Real Deals Mag., Supply Management Mag., People Management Mag. Further examples of Pablo's work can be found in his extensive folio online at www.debutart.com

Cover for Rumbos Magazine. Article about Argentinian inventors.

Portrait of Rocky Balboa. From Pablo Bernasconi's Portrait Book. (Edhasa – 2008).

For Clarin Newspaper. Article about Writer's Teachers.

For Clubhouse Magazine. Article about Family Holidays.

Cover for Caras y Caretas Magazine. Article about Plaza de Mayo's history.

Comm. by Wieden + Kennedy for Nokia headphones ads.

193

Nick Reddyhoff

Début Art & The Coningsby Gallery
30 Tottenham Street
London W1T 4RJ
UK

☎ + 44 (0)20 7636 1064
☎ + 44 (0)20 7636 7478
🖷 + 44 (0)20 7580 7017
✉ info@debutart.com
🌐 www.debutart.com

Nick's unique visual style and approach is attracting a wide range of leading clients worldwide.

Previous clients incl: The Grammys, Heineken, Steljes, Billboard Mag., FHM, Prudential Health, Unilever, Abbey, Caterpillar, NatWest, The IOD, Vauxhall, Cadbury's,

The Times, Aberdeen Univ., Caspian Publ., Future Publ., John Brown Publ., MediaMark, Dennis Publ., Community Care Magazine.

Further examples of Nick's work can be viewed on page 190 in Contact 21 and in his extensive folio on the web at www.debutart.com

the coningsby gallery

Comm. by Pride Magazine for article about ethnic recruitment to the Prison Service.

Justin Timberlake. Comm. by Redezine for the 49th Grammy Awards Programme Book.

Steve Jobs, CEO of Apple. Comm. by Billboard Magazine.

Red Mist

Début Art & The Coningsby Gallery
30 Tottenham Street
London W1T 4RJ
UK

☎ + 44 (0)20 7636 1064
☎ + 44 (0)20 7636 7478
📠 + 44 (0)20 7580 7017
✉ info@debutart.com
🌐 www.debutart.com

Red Mist's style and approach has been attracting assignments from a wide range of leading clients worldwide.

Previous clients include: Prudential Insurance, Tequila, Eon, British Gas, Gala Casinos, The Conrad Davies Company, The Radio Times, Caspian Magazine Publishing.

Further examples of Red Mist's work can be found in his extensive folio online at www.debutart.com

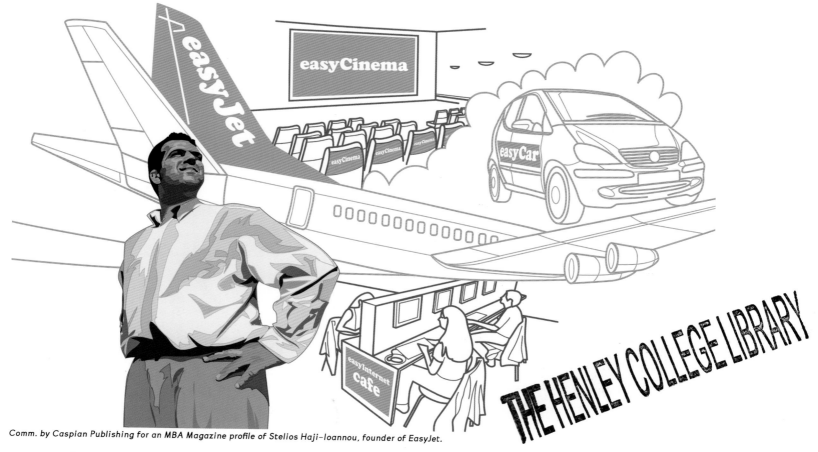

Comm. by Caspian Publishing for an MBA Magazine profile of Stelios Haji-Ioannou, founder of EasyJet.

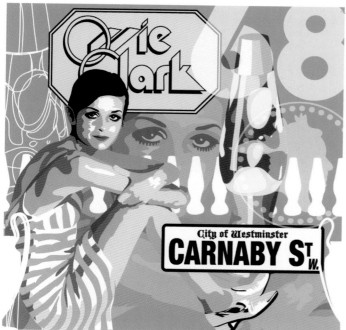

'1968.' Comm. by The Conrad Davies Company for Manchester Utd plc. Celebrating the 1968 European Cup Winner's Cup win. (Two of nine images. 120 x 120cm panels).

195

Sarah Hanson

Début Art & The Coningsby Gallery
30 Tottenham Street
London W1T 4RJ
UK

T + 44 (0)20 7636 1064
T + 44 (0)20 7636 7478
F + 44 (0)20 7580 7017
E info@debutart.com
W www.debutart.com

Sarah graduated from the University of Hertfordshire with a First class Honours degree in Graphic Design and illustration. Her photo-collages combine traditional with digital techniques, using hand drawn elements, photographs, and found ephemera. Her illustrations reflect her passion for surface, pattern, retro design and nostalgia.

Previous clients incl:
British Airways, The Times, BBC Worldwide, Caspian Publ., GQ Mag., The Practical Law Company, The Radio Times, More Mag. (US), Investor Relations Mag., Waitrose Food Illustrated, Age Concern.

www.debutart for full online portfolio.

Comm. by BA Highlife Mag. For feature on Bill Bryson.

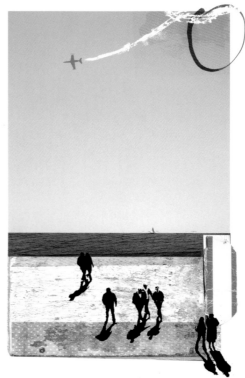

'Holidays'. Self-directed work.

'The Migrant'. Self-directed work.

Book Cover. Comm. by Penguin for 'On The Road' by Jack Kerouac.

Arno

Début Art & The Coningsby Gallery
30 Tottenham Street
London W1T 4RJ
UK

☎ + 44 (0)20 7636 1064
☎ + 44 (0)20 7636 7478
📠 + 44 (0)20 7580 7017
✉ info@debutart.com
🌐 www.debutart.com

"Hyper-realism" is used for paintings that "look just like photographs". I create digital illustrations that look realistic yet definitely "painted". It's not a picture, it's not 3D, in fact it's a bit of both...

I've worked my way from Lucasfilms Ltd. to Jim Henson Creature Shop with a detour by Marvel, DC Comics, and Chanel.

Other previous clients incl: Coca-Cola, Penguin Books, HedKandi, MTV, Sony Playstation 2 & 3, Dubai Air Show, Shockwave, Toni&Guy, Maxim (USA), The Sunday Times, Mojo Mag., Men's Fitness Mag., FHM Mag.

Further examples of Arno's work can be found in his extensive portfolio on the web at at www.debutart.com

the coningsby gallery

Comm. by SONY for SingStar Playstation 3 Game wallpaper.

Beach House Album cover for HedKandi.

Suzy Sioux as 'Wicked Queen'. Comm. by Mojo Magazine.

Oliver Burston

Début Art & The Coningsby Gallery
30 Tottenham Street
London W1T 4RJ
UK

☎ + 44 (0)20 7636 1064
☎ + 44 (0)20 7636 7478
📠 + 44 (0)20 7580 7017
✉ info@debutart.com
🌐 www.debutart.com

Oliver's outstanding brand of high resolution visual imagery, coupled with his reputation for making experienced and finely judged inputs to briefs continues to attract leading clients seeking distinctive solutions all over the world. Oliver enjoys working at the cutting edge of digital technology, employing the latest advances in 2D & 3D visualisation. Previous clients incl; David Bowie, George Lucas, Michael Jackson, MTV, Ford, Sony, Fuji, BA, Mars, BT, BMW, IBM, NatWest Bank, The Design Council, Hellmanns, BP, Harper Collins, Egmont Books, Orion Books, The FT, The Times, The Independent on Sunday, The Observer, Focus Mag., Nature Mag, Focus Mag, Men's Health Mag, Men's Fitness Mag. More examples of Oliver's work can be found on p160–161 in Contact 23 and in his extensive folio on the web at www.debutart.com

the coningsby gallery

Comm. by Public Finance Magazine.

Comm. by Summersault for Siemens Mag article about world ecology.

Comm. by New Electronics Mag for article about new teaching practice.

Front cover for a Euromoney Magazine article about the Green Economy.

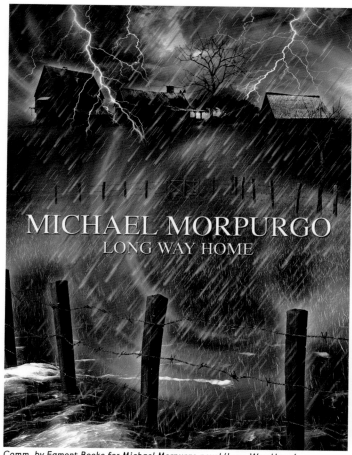

Comm. by Egmont Books for Michael Morpurgo novel 'Long Way Home'.

Cover image for The Banker Magazine. Events issue.

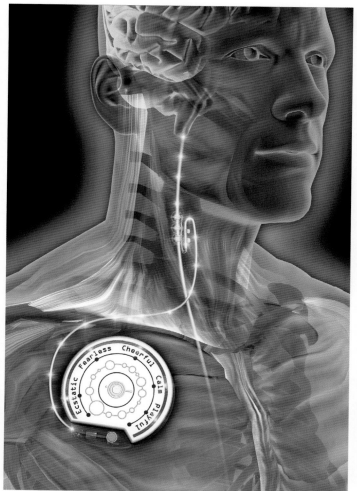

Comm. by BBC Focus Mag for article about Neurological Mood Enhancers.

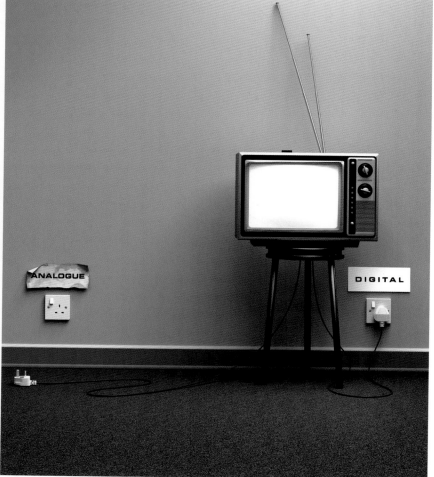

Cover for Inside Housing Mag. Digital Switchover article.

RealtimeUK

RealtimeUK London
212 Piccadilly
London W1J 9HG
UK

T + 44 (0)20 7830 9310
E info@realtimeuk.com
W www.realtimeuk.com
W www.contact-me.net/Realtime

RealtimeUK North
Willows Farm Studios
Ballam Road
Westby
Lancashire PR4 3PN
UK

T + 44 (0)1772 682 363
F + 44 (0)1772 683 592

Our clients: Audi, THQ, BAE SYSTEMS,
Sony Computer Entertainment Europe,
Fiat, Evolution Studios, Jaguar,
Juice Games, LG, Codemasters.

Please see previous Contact editons:
14–23.

realtime:uk

realtime:uk

Third Edge Ltd

17a Riding House Street
London W1W 7DS
UK

☎ + 44 (0)20 7436 7930
✉ info@the3rdedge.com
🌐 www.the3rdedge.com
🌐 www.contact-me.net/ThirdEdge

Fast, responsive and good quality. Third Edge Studio can meet all your needs, from highly photorealistic 3D illustration to fast turn around visuals to boost your pitching ideas. We house various styles of illustration, and our artwork service can help take your ideas from concepts through to finished print. With the inclusion of large format printing, mockups and video virals to our name, Third Edge truly has it all your creative needs covered.

Peter Hutchinson

25 Cranmore Gardens
Belfast
Co Antrim BT9 6LJ
Northern Ireland
UK

T + 44 (0)28 9066 8205
F + 44 (0)28 9066 3594
M + 44 (0)7768 435 888
E design@peterhutchinson.org
W www.peterhutchinson.org

I specialise in fine line, pen and ink drawings, either black and white or full colour, especially aerial views and perspective dawings of streetscapes and urban scenes.

My style ranges from the quick freehand sketch to detailed hard line drawings. I have a flexible and open approach to my illustrative work.

I ensure it is delivered on time and to budget.

Additional samples of my illustrations are available on request.

Also for further examples of my work have a look at:

Contact 16, 17, 21, 22 & 23 and AOI Images 25 & 31 publications.

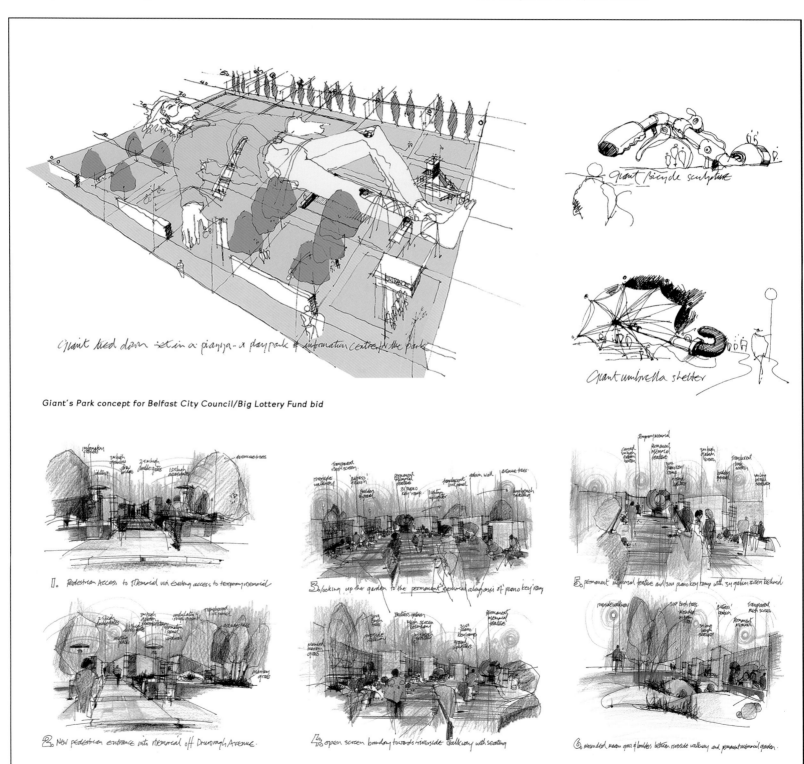

Giant's Park concept for Belfast City Council/Big Lottery Fund bid

Omagh Bomb Memorial design competition/Visual Journey

Marina Caruso

Début Art & The Coningsby Gallery
30 Tottenham Street
London W1T 4RJ
UK

☎ + 44 (0)20 7636 1064
☎ + 44 (0)20 7636 7478
📠 + 44 (0)20 7580 7017
✉ info@debutart.com
🌐 www.debutart.com

Marina's unique mix of freehand, photography and on-system work is attracting a wide range of clients in the advertising, design, editorial and entertainment sectors worldwide.

Previous clients include:
VisitLondon, Zipit (USA), Seamless Recordings, Digital River, The FT, Legal & General, Marie-Claire, Time Out, The Guardian, Toni & Guy, Sunday Express, New Scientist, Waitrose Food Illustrated, The London Magazine, Edizioni Selecta Publ.

More examples of Marina's work can be viewed on page 148-149 in Contact 23 and in her extensive portfolio on-line at www.debutart.com

the coningsby gallery

'Spanish Wine by Region'. Comm. by Waitrose Food Illustrated Magazine.

'Fear of Flying'. Comm. by Sunday Times Travel supplement.

One of a series of images for Zipit (USA).

Vincent Wakerley

iD2 Studio
Country House
Sea End Road
Benington
Lincolnshire PE22 0DQ
UK

☎ + 44 (0)1205 761 793
📱 + 44 (0)7801 766 863
✉ vincentwakerley@btinternet.com
🌐 www.vincentwakerley.com

Slick and highly finished digital photo-illustration for product packaging, advertising and publishing. Extensive website portfolio. Call or email Vincent to discuss your project.

Bill Ledger

17 Towncourt Crescent
Petts Wood
Kent BR5 1PG
UK

T + 44 (0)1689 821 383
M + 44 (0)7929 171966
E studio@billledger.com
W www.billledger.com
W www.contact-me.net/BillLedger

Full animation service
2D 3D Flash interactive
ToyBox Animation
www.toyboxanimation.co.uk
info@toyboxanimation.co.uk

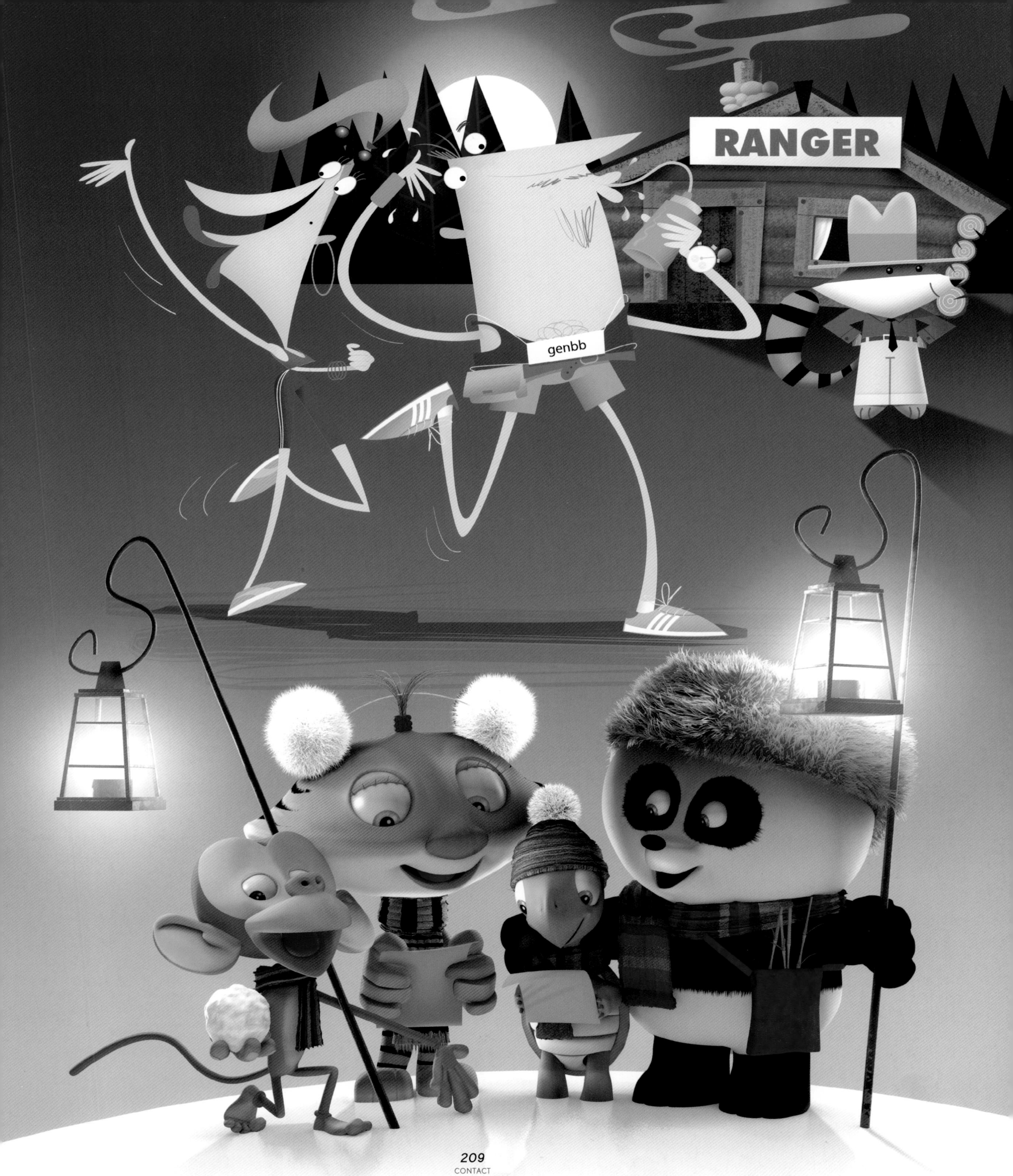
RANGER
genbb

Jackdaw

Début Art & The Coningsby Gallery
30 Tottenham Street
London W1T 4RJ
UK

☎ + 44 (0)20 7636 1064
☎ + 44 (0)20 7636 7478
🖷 + 44 (0)20 7580 7017
✉ info@debutart.com
🌐 www.debutart.com

Jackdaw creates highly contemporary and imaginative imagery, attracting a wide range of clients worldwide. Jackdaw's work combines both freehand and photographic elements for use in all forms of media. Jackdaw conduct their own photography and can also work with client supplied material.

Previous clients include: Diageo (UDV Classic Malt Whiskies), BP, Honda, Volkswagen, The Royal Opera House, NCR, LucasFilms (USA), Scholastic/Disney (USA), Random House (UK and USA), Harper Collins (UK and USA), Kenco, NASDAQ, 3i plc, NTT Telecom, The LSE, NatWest Bank, Orion Publ., Penguin Books, New Scientist, The FT.

Further examples of Jackdaw's work can be found on-line at www.debutart.com

the coningsby gallery

Personal piece.

Comm. by Deep for Vicinitee Magazine front cover.

Commissioned by major UK ad agency for global telecoms company.

All images on this page are personal pieces.

Sarah J Coleman

UK

T + 44 (0)1455 632 819
M + 44 (0)7941 279 374
E sarah@inkymole.com
W www.inkymole.com
W www.contact-me.net/SarahColeman

Putting ink on paper for
McCann Erickson, Joshua G2,
J Walter Thompson, Walker Books,
Isobel, Leo Burnett,
Channel 4, MBA, Egmont,
Epitaph Records and lots of others.

Enquiring from the USA? Do contact
the lovely people at Bernstein and
Andriulli, New York:
http://www.ba-reps.com

It's the summer holidays and Amber is bored. Then everything changes when she meets Dowdie, a non-conformist who draws Amber into a world of dark and dangerous secrets . . . secrets of the Amethyst Children.

A gripping contemporary novel about a cult, from an acclaimed new author.

www.simonsays.co.uk

SIMON AND SCHUSTER
£6.99

Illustration by Sarah Coleman
Design by Nick Stearn

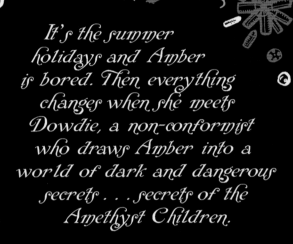
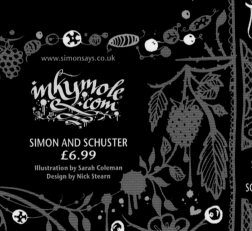

Sarah Singleton · The Amethyst Child

SIMON
AND
SCHUSTER

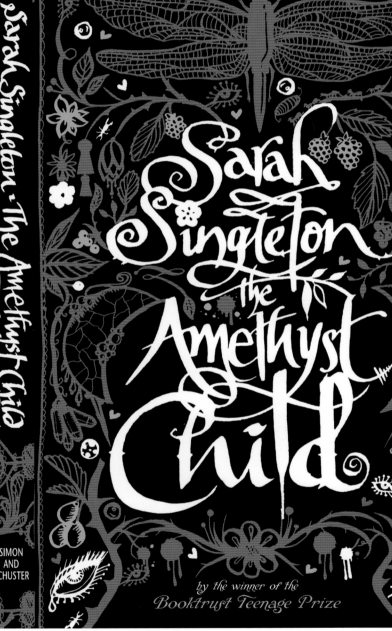

Sarah Singleton
the Amethyst Child

by the winner of the
Booktrust Teenage Prize

The Organisation

UK Office

☎ 0845 054 8033 (UK only)
☎ + 44 (0)20 7833 8268
🖷 + 44 (0)20 7833 8269
📱 + 44 (0)7973 172 902
✉ info@organisart.co.uk
🌐 www.organisart.co.uk
🌐 www.contact-me.net/TheOrganisation

New York Office

Pauline Mason

☎ + 1 917 586 6514
✉ masonpmac@yahoo.com

Over 70 portfolios online –
Cutting edge international image
makers.
Search by
Style – Medium – Subject Matter
Large Stock Library online –
Easy solutions to impossible deadlines
Purchase your favourite artwork –
www.illustrationgallery.co.uk

the organisation

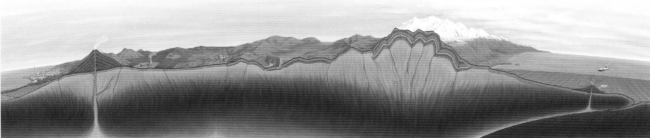

Chris Davidson

0845 054 8033   www.organisart.co.uk   info@organisart.co.uk

Domanic Li

Deborah van de Leijgraaf

Ingela Peterson

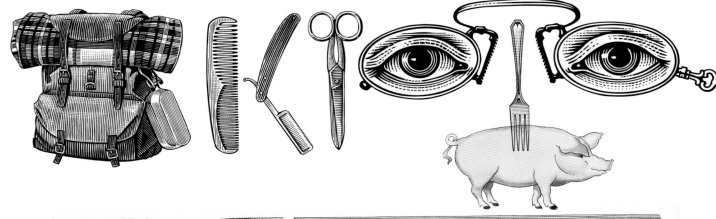

Fred van Deelen

Lorna Siviter

Richard Johnson

0845 054 8033 www.organisart.co.uk info@organisart.co.uk

Natacha Ledwidge

Paul Oakley

London
UK

☎ *+ 44 (0)7931 717 097*
✉ *paulogandi@hotmail.com*
🌐 *www.paulogandi.com*
🌐 *www.contact-me.net/PaulOakley*

Recent clients include:
Mastercard, Filofax, Virgin,
Clarins, Natori, So Good Milk,
Radio Times, OUP, Scholastic,
IPC, Hachette Filipacci,
Condé Naste, The Express,
The Telegraph.

See Contact 17–23.

Paul Oakley

T + 44 (0)7931 717 097

mr-dunn* studio

Oakwood House
70 Inkerman Drive
Hazlemere
Buckinghamshire HP15 7JJ
UK

☎ + 44 (0)1494 714 993
📱 + 44 (0)7970 855 958
✉ mrdunn236@hotmail.com
🌐 www.mr-dunn.com
🌐 www.contact-me.net/GaryDunn

Established for 20 years, mr-dunn* studio specialises in unique character development and character based illustrations for packaging, print and advertising.
We also get involved in production design for commercial campaigns, children's books (both fictional & educational) and comic strips.
We hope you like what you see, give us a call to see if we can help you.

See our updated website for 2007
www.mr-dunn.com

Also in Contact 23 page 153
22 pg 27
21 pg 24
20 pg 13
19 pg 84
18 pg 55
17 pg 28
16 pg 87

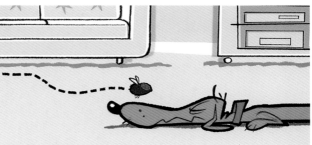

Nick Diggory

UK

T + 44 (0)1606 784 396
F + 44 (0)1606 784 533
E nick@nickdiggory.com
W www.nickdiggory.com
W www.contact-me.net/NickDiggory

Harry Malt

Début Art & The Coningsby Gallery
30 Tottenham Street
London W1T 4RJ
UK

T + 44 (0)20 7636 1064
T + 44 (0)20 7636 7478
F + 44 (0)20 7580 7017
E info@debutart.com
W www.debutart.com

By stylistically approaching each project without entrenched pre-conceived ideas, I aim to create work that is unique and honestly suited to my client's particular needs. I like to retain a playfulness throughout my work which adds accessibility and enjoyment. The brief will determine the media I use.
Previous clients incl: The Royal Mail, Virgin, Volvo, Puma, HSBC, Capital One, Hill & Knowlton, Cadbury's, B&Q, IBM, Microsoft, The Consumer Association, Single Homeless Project, Assoc. for the Indigenous Peoples of the Americas (AIPA), VH1, NME, Sky, HHCL, JWT, Dazed & Confused, Notting Hill Film Festival, BigLife Record Co.

More examples of my work can be found in my extensive portfolio at www.debutart.com

the coningsby gallery

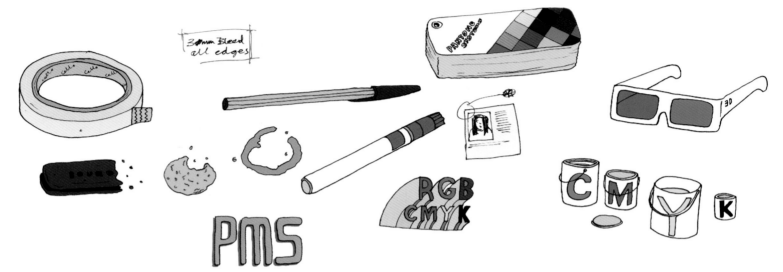

'Sending Work to Print'. Comm. by Digit Magazine.

'Santa Letter'. Comm. by FHM for Christmas 'Debt' issue.

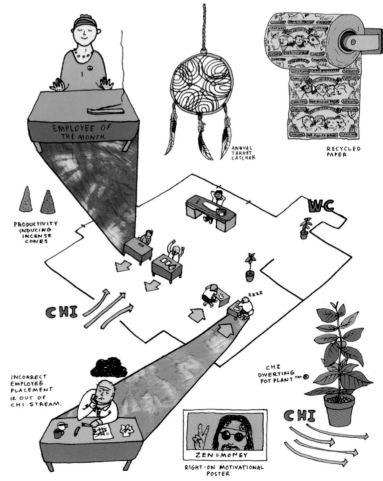

Comm. by OnOffice Mag. for an article about Office Feng Shui.

'Stock Transfers'. Comm. by Inside Housing Magazine for an article on Stock Transfer.

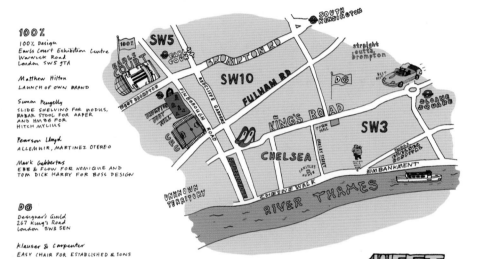

FIND OUT WHERE THE DESIGNERS
IN OUR COVER STORY WILL BE
SHOWING DURING LONDON'S
DESIGN WEEK...

100%
100% Design
Earls Court Exhibition Centre
Warwick Road
London SW5 9TA

Matthew Hilton
LAUNCH OF OWN BRAND

Simon Pengelly
SLIDE SHELVING FOR MODUS,
BABAR STOOL FOR ARPER
AND HM86 FOR
HITCH MYLIUS

Pearson Lloyd
ALLERMUIR, MARTINEZ OTERO

Mark Gabbertas
EBB & FLOW FOR NOMIQUE AND
TOM DICK HARRY FOR BOSS DESIGN

DG
Designer's Guild
267 King's Road
London SW3 5EN

Klauser & Carpenter
EASY CHAIR FOR ESTABLISHED & SONS

Design Week map. Comm. by One AD for OnOffice Magazine.

Comm. by Digit Magazine for an article about Pantone.

Comm. by McCann-Erickson (London) for their own branding and website.

Glen McBeth

4 Abbey Mains Cottages
Haddington
East Lothian
EH41 3SB
UK

T + 44 (0)1620 824 025
M + 44 (0)7713 590 498
E email@glenmcbeth.co.uk
W www.glenmcbeth.co.uk
W www.contact-me.net/GlenMcBeth

Recent clients include:

The Wellcome Trust
BBC History Magazine
Chambers Harrap Publishing
Crieff Hydro Hotel
Campbell & Co Design
The National Trust for Scotland

Shaw Design
Learn Direct Scotland
The City of Edinburgh Council
Fife Council

See also:
page 103 Contact 22
page 167 Contact 21

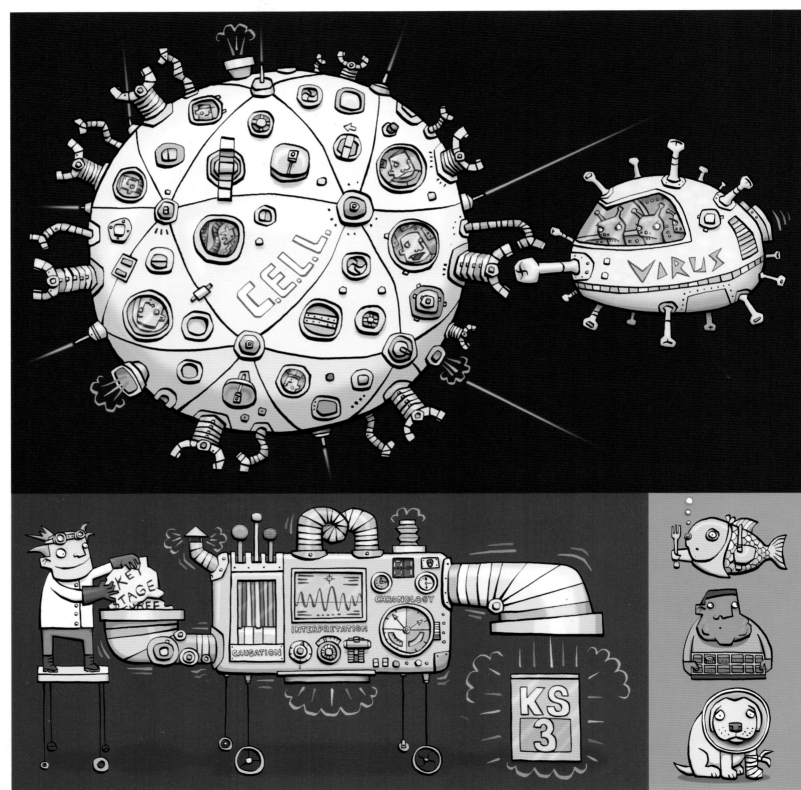

Andy Parker

The Meadows
Firgrove Road
Whitehill
Hampshire GU35 9DY
UK

☎ + 44 (0)1420 487 735
✉ mail@andyparker-illustrator.co.uk
🌐 www.andyparker-illustrator.co.uk
🌐 www.contact-me.net/AndyParker

Please visit my online portfolio or call for samples.

See also Contact Illustrators 11 to 23.

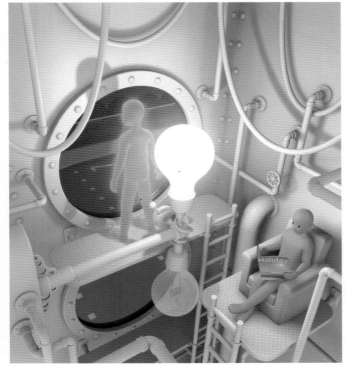

John Bradley

67 Highfield Road
Newbold
Chesterfield
Derbyshire S41 7HS
UK

☎ + 44 (0)1246 238953
📧 johnbillustrator@btopenworld.com
🌐 www.johnbradleyillustrator.com
🌐 www.contact-me.net/JohnBradley

Clients include The Guardian, The Observer, Men's Health, Easyjet, English Symphony Orchestra, Northern Broadsides Theatre Company, Pan Macmillan, Oxford University Press, Local Government Chronicle, Manchester United, Pearson Education, the BBC, Times Educational Supplement, Autocar, plus many, many more over the last eighteen years.

CGA Magazine

Pearson Education

WPT Magazine

Money Observer

Jo Brown

UK

T + 44 (0)7966 134 342
E jo@jo-brown.co.uk
W www.jo-brown.co.uk
W www.contact-me.net/JoBrown

See also: Contacts 14–22

Jan Lewis

1 Coombe End
Whitchurch Hill
Pangbourne
Berkshire RG8 7PD
UK

📞 + 44 (0)118 984 2590
✉ jan.lewis1@btinternet.com
🌐 www.contact-me.net/JanLewis

I'm quite versatile but I enjoy
children's books best, all ages, bright,
washy colour or black and white.

Publishers I have worked for include...
Walker books, Hodder, Orchard,
Macmillan, Kingfisher, Harper Collins,
Egmont, Lion, Heinneman, Parragon,
OUP, Cornelsen and BBC TV.

Barry Downard

Début Art & The Coningsby Gallery
30 Tottenham Street
London W1T 4RJ
UK

☎ + 44 (0)20 7636 1064
☎ + 44 (0)20 7636 7478
🖷 + 44 (0)20 7580 7017
✉ info@debutart.com
🖳 www.debutart.com

Barry's unique combination of CGI, photo–montage, photo–collage and illustration is attracting high profile assignment work from leading clients in the fields of advertising, design, magazine and book publishing worldwide.
Previous clients incl: BMW–Mini, Bacardi, Orangina, SAAB, Nestlé, Ola, Cleveland Opera (USA), Simon and Schuster Books, Time Warner Books,

Omnibus Books, SONY Playstation, Glaxo Smith Kline, The Arizona Opera, De Beers, Sun International, Empire Magazine, The Economist, Euromoney Mag., Men's Health Mag., Men's Fitness Mag, New Electronics Mag, Machinery Mag., Eureka Mag.

More examples of Barry's work can be found online in his folio on the web at www.debutart.com

the coningsby gallery

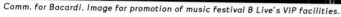

Comm. for Bacardi. Image for promotion of music festival B Live's VIP facilities.

'Doug's Topiary Garden'. Self–initiated piece.

Comm. for Orangina for bus–backs by TBWA Energy Manchester.

'Exploding Citroën'. Comm. by Men's Health Mag. for article 'Seven Blunders of the Modern World' about the dangers of excessive earphone use.

Annabel Tempest

Tempest Creative Ltd
Darracott
Wiltown
Curry Rivel, Langport
Somerset TA10 OJF
UK

T + 44 (0)1458 251 042
M + 44 (0)7939 289 647
E annabel.tempest@virgin.net
W www.contact-me.net/AnnabelTempest

My work ranges from children's book illustration and greeting cards to editorial and advertising.

Further examples of my work can be found in Contact 16–23.

Simon Farr

41 Park Road
Aldeburgh
Suffolk IP15 5EN
UK

☎ + 44 (0)1728 452 486
📱 + 44 (0)7749 890 353
✉ farout@btinternet.com
🌐 www.simonfarr.co.uk
🌐 www.contact-me.net/SimonFarr

Illustrations, cartoons, portraits and caricatures using pen, ink and watercolour.

Work delivered by email to tight deadlines with good humour.

Recent clients include:
The Guardian (irregular political cartoons), Daily Mail (weekly), Sunday Times (sometimes),

Public Finance Magazine (monthly), Easyjet (once) and numerous other publications and designers.

See also Contact no's 22, 20, 16, 15, 14.

Sunday Times Worldwide Supplement – after Carravaggio

Annabel Milne

Grooms Cottage
Elsenham Hall
Elsenham
Nr Bishops Stortford
Herts CM22 6DP
UK

☏ + 44 (0)1279 814 923
📱 + 44 (0)7890 992 654
✉ annabel@a-milne.demon.co.uk
🌐 www.contact-me.net/AnnabelMilne

Medical and General Illustration including research, anatomical work, explanatory diagrams, flora & fauna etc. Illustrations can be supplied as either conventional or computer generated artwork.

Illustration Collection:
I also hold a collection of my illustrations, which are available for license.

See also:
Contact 14 pages 98–99
Contact 15 pages 334–335
Contact 16 page 283
Contact 17 pages 406–407
Contact 18 pages 514–515
Contact 19 pages 390–391
Contact 20 pages 450–451
Contact 21 pages 70–71
Contact 22 pages 166–167
Contact 23 pages 266–267

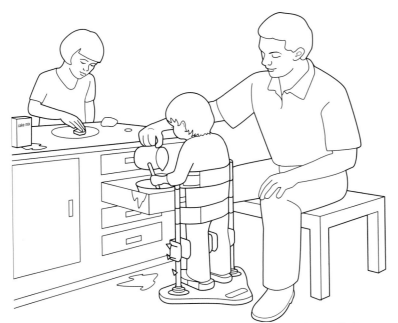

Computer generated illustration showing 'The Marie Stopes Partnership' for Marie Stopes International and an illustration titled 'Learning to Cook Together' from Handling the Young Child with Cerebral Palsy at Home.

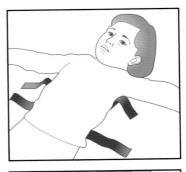

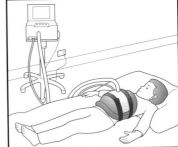

Computer generated illustration showing 'The Application of Cuirass' from Children in Intensive Care a Survival Guide.

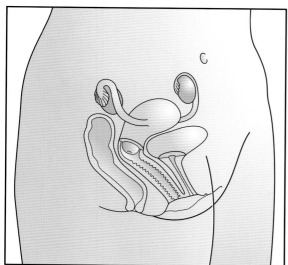

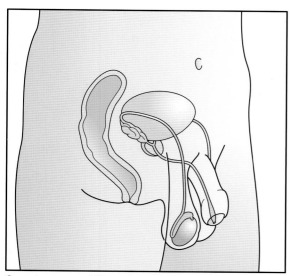

Computer generated illustrations showing 'Young Girl with Acne' from Precocious Puberty and 'Male and Female Reproductive Organs' for The Right to Life Charitable Trust.

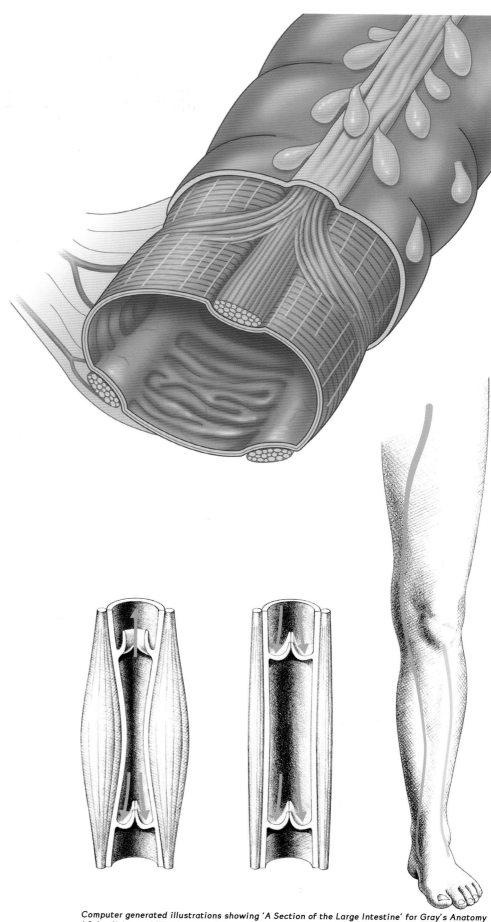

Computer generated illustrations showing 'A Section of the Large Intestine' for Gray's Anatomy 40th edition and 'The Position of Long and Short Saphenous Vein' and 'Normal Valve Operation' for Origin Medical Vein Clinic.

Octagon Computer Graphics

The Pheasants
Lynn Road
Middleton, King's Lynn
Norfolk PE32 1RQ
UK

T + 44 (0)1553 841 897
F + 44 (0)1553 841 307
M + 44 (0)7887 983 123
E alex@octagongraphics.co.uk
W www.contact-me.net/OctagonGraphics

High quality computer-generated photorealistic visuals, animations and technical illustrations to promote new concepts or existing products. A range of subjects are covered such as Packaging, Transport, Medical, Technical and Architectural. Very fast turnaround, often with very short notice and very tight deadlines, working directly with international clients as well as countrywide in the UK.

Clients include:
Barclays Bank, Britvic, Cadbury's, Cobra Beer, Coca-Cola, Interbrew, JVC, McVities, Nestlé, Vauxhall.

Please see the website for more examples or contact Alex for a DVD showreel.

Octagon Computer Graphics
3D Visualisation & Illustration

Rebecca Sutherland

1 Morton Gardens
Wallington
Surrey SM6 8EU
UK

☎ + 44 (0)20 8714 3322
📱 + 44 (0)7801 969 549
✉ beck.jim@blueyonder.co.uk
🌐 www.rebeccasutherland.co.uk
🌐 www.contact-me.net/RebeccaSutherland

Collage and paper cuts

Clients include:
BigTop design
Hat-trick design
London Illustrated News Group
Orient Express Magazine
Pearson Education
Penguin Books
Royal Mail

Glyn Goodwin

The Drawing Room
38 Mount Pleasant
London WC1 XOAP
UK

T + 44 (0)20 7833 1335
F + 44 (0)20 7833 3064
M + 44 (0)7946 619 005
E glyngoodwin@hotmail.com
W www.glyngoodwin.co.uk
W www.contact-me.net/GlynGoodwin

Clients include BBC, Heinemann,
Hodder, Canning, Weekend FT,
Archant, Sunday Mirror,
The Eton Collection, Zion Hill, OUP,
Square Seven and Visible Edge
amongst many others.

Espresso Animation

5th Floor
Century House
100 Oxford Street
London W1D 1LN
Uk

T + 44 (0)20 7637 9090
F + 44 (0)20 7637 9339
M + 44 (0)7720 074 804
E philip@espressoanimation.com
W www.espressoanimation.com

Espresso Animation director, Philip Vallentin, says:
"It's always fun to have some appeal in the characters regardless of how the image is created."

More than twenty years of animation experience. That's a lot of scribbling, doodling and colouring in.

Loose or tight, drawn freehand, or computer-assisted, solo effort or group input, it's all to do with expression and personality.

Guaranteed, one free espresso with every job!

The Organisation

UK Office

📞 0845 054 8033 (UK only)
📞 + 44 (0)20 7833 8268
📠 + 44 (0)20 7833 8269
📱 + 44 (0)7973 172 902
✉ info@organisart.co.uk
🌐 www.organisart.co.uk
🌐 www.contact-me.net/TheOrganisation

New York Office

Pauline Mason

📞 + 1 917 586 6514
✉ masonpmac@yahoo.com

Over 70 portfolios online –
Cutting edge international image
makers.
Search by
Style – Medium – Subject Matter
Large Stock Library online –
Easy solutions to impossible deadlines
Purchase your favourite artwork –
www.illustrationgallery.co.uk

Graham Evernden

Alison Jay

the organisation

0845 054 8033   www.organisart.co.uk   info@organisart.co.uk

the organisation

0845 054 8033   www.organisart.co.uk   info@organisart.co.uk

Mark Ruffle

0845 054 8033 www.organisart.co.uk info@organisart.co.uk

THE GUARDIAN

COMPUTER ACTIVE MAGAZINE

a boy called ELVIS

X360 MAGAZINE

a boy called MICHAEL

POPJUSTICE BOOKS
THE FRIDAY PROJECT

essential guide to moving abroad

OPTV MAGAZINE

FAN BANTA
Where fans get their kicks

X360 MAGAZINE

FANBANTA.COM

David Whittle

JavierJoaquin

Javier Joaquin

Ruth Rivers

Sophie Rohrbach

Finger Industries Ltd

Site Gallery
1 Brown Street
Sheffield S1 2BS
UK

T + 44 (0)1142 724 777
F + 44 (0)1142 812 078
M + 44 (0)7974 578 885
E us@fingerindustries.co.uk
W www.fingerindustries.co.uk
W www.contact-me.net/FingerIndustries

Imaginative, original, experienced, and committed to making clients happy.

Also see Contacts 20 to 23.

Character design, 2D and 3D animation design and production, editorial, publishing and advertising illustration.

Clients:
Lloyds TSB, TMW, Rainey Kelly CR/Y&R, Hamleys of London, WARL, Brahm, Random House, Tesco, Hodder Headline, Guardian Weekend, Bank of Scotland, Scottish Media Group, Sunday Times, HSBC and more.

Contact:
Marcus Kenyon or Jonny Ford

'Political Animals'

'Rudelf' – © PriceRunner AB/TMW 2007

Red Band Sweets © Leaf UK/WARL 2007

'The Family That Skates Together,
Stays Together'

Sony animation concept

© LloydsTSB 2007

© LloydsTSB 2007

Red Band Sweets – 30' TV Ad © Leaf UK/WARL 2007

Ned Jolliffe

79d Oxford Gardens
London W10 5UL
UK

☎ + 44 (0)20 8964 8231
📱 + 44 (0)7772 678 772
✉ ned.j@mac.com
🌐 www.misterned.com
🌐 www.contact-me.net/NedJolliffe

Represented by:
Eye Candy Illustration

☎ + 44 (0)20 8291 0729
☎ + 44 (0)1889 504 411 (24hrs)
🌐 www.eyecandy.co.uk

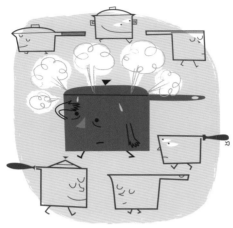

1 IN 7 BRITISH ADULTS HAVE **HIGH BLOOD PRESSURE**

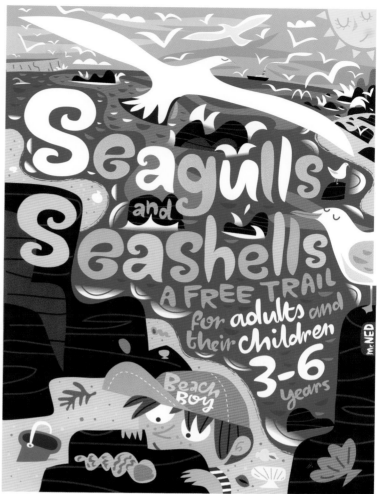

Dylan Gibson Illustration

Scotland
UK

☎ + 44 (0)1796 470 392
📱 + 44 (0)7762 354 784
✉ info@dylangibsonillustration.co.uk
🌐 www.dylangibsonillustration.co.uk
🌐 www.contact-me.net/DylanGibson

A fresh approach to illustration.
Work to date includes: advertising,
comics, character design, editorial,
educational imagery, fashion
and storyboards.

Clients include:
BBC Worldwide, Clarks, The Guardian,
Oxford University Press and Tesco.

To view samples and learn more call
or visit my website.

Represented by Eye Candy Illustration
Agency. Member of the AOI.

Jill Calder

UK

T + 44 (0)1333 313 737
M + 44 (0)7881 520 662
E jill@jillcalder.com
W www.jillcalder.com
W www.contact-me.net/JillCalder

Clients include:
Siemens, Target USA
Random House
Neiman Marcus
Mass Mutual
B&Q, Food & Wine
The British Council
Wacom Europe
The New Yorker
Philip Morris, ICAS
Harvard Business Review

Pan Macmillan
Polygon Books
Homes & Interiors Scotland
Absolute New York
The Guardian
UCLA, SKYY Vodka
and many more.

Also see page 141 in Contact 21,
page 34 in Contact 22 and page 35
in Contact 23.

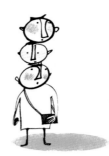

Ian Bull

27 Forthbridge Road
Battersea
London SW11 5NX
UK

☎ + 44 (0)20 7223 3572
✉ ianbull@btinternet.com
🌐 www.precisionartwork.co.uk
🌐 www.contact-me.net/IanBull

Everything you see here was created using resolution-independent vector graphics, as has most of my work during the past 18 years.
An extensive portfolio is available which, besides general illustration, includes packaging, exhibition design, cartography and security stationery.

There are also videos and 'quicktime movies' of recent television commercials.

You see, I'm not entirely limited to railways!

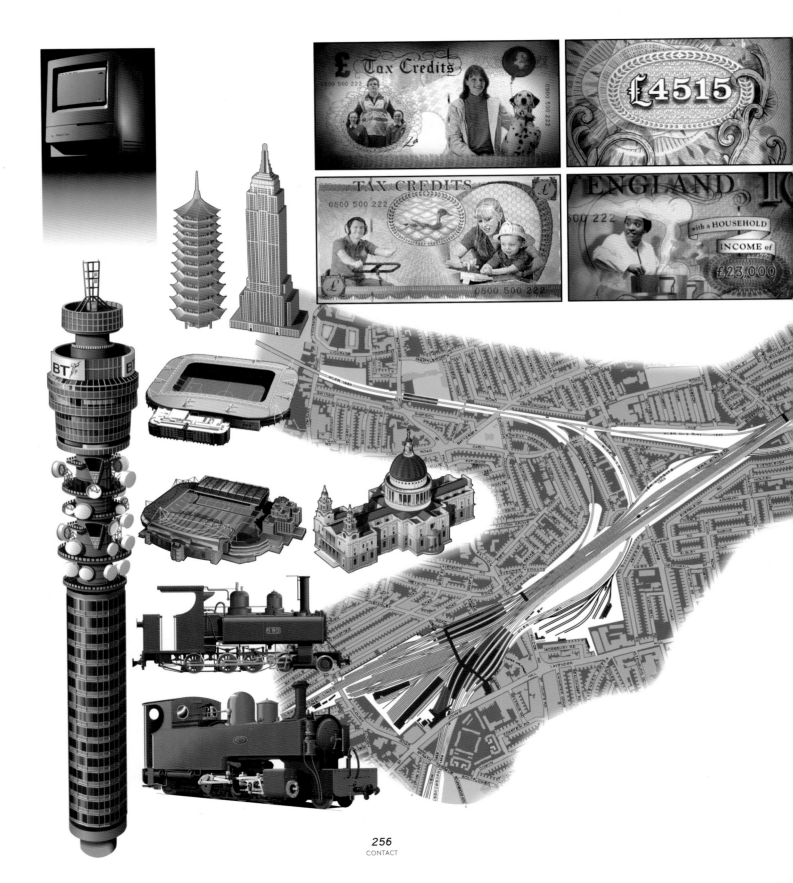

Matt Herring

Début Art & The Coningsby Gallery
30 Tottenham Street
London W1T 4RJ
UK

☎ + 44 (0)20 7636 1064
☎ + 44 (0)20 7636 7478
📠 + 44 (0)20 7580 7017
✉ info@debutart.com
🌐 www.debutart.com

Matt's unique on-system achieved photo-collage illustration style attracts clients worldwide. Matt works extensively in the advertising, design and magazine editorial fields.
Previous clients incl: Honda, Nike, BA, MTV, Bacardi, Peugeot, The Royal Mail, HSBC, Virgin, The BBC, Toyota, Design Week, BP, Timeout, Top Gear, Penguin, 5 Live, The Times, Shell, HarperCollins, Now Mag., Cisco Systems, Marie Claire Mag., The FT, Computer Arts, Which?, NASDAQ, Esquire, Business Week, Waterstones, Sainsbury's, Corvette, IBM, The RAC, The Independent, Jeep, Classic FM, Mojo, New Scientist, Men's Health, The Guardian, The Economist, The Observer, Red Mag., The Harvard Business Review.
More examples of Matt's work can be found in his extensive portfolio on the web at www.debutart.com

the coningsby gallery

'Celebrity Blogs'. Commissioned by The Sunday Telegraph Magazine.

75th Anniversary image for The BBC World Service.

'Work/Life balance'. Comm. by Healthy Magazine.

Comm. by Penguin Books for cover of book 'Ripley's Game.'

75th Anniversary image for The BBC World Service.

Myles Talbot

3 Sunnydale Park
East Morton
Keighley
West Yorkshire BD20 5UF
UK

T + 44 (0)1274 510 338
M + 44 (0)7710 831 288
E myles@mylestalbot.com
W www.mylestalbot.com
W www.contact-me.net/MylesTalbot

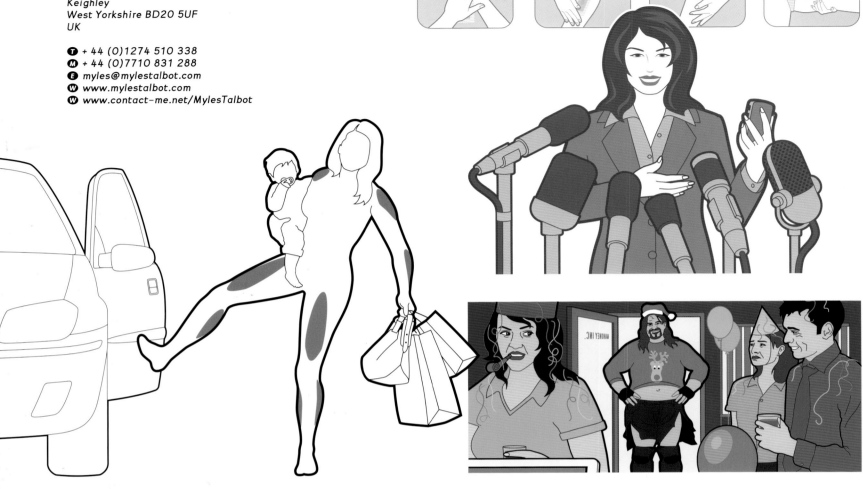

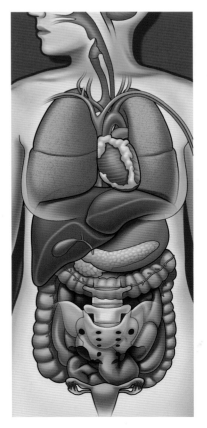

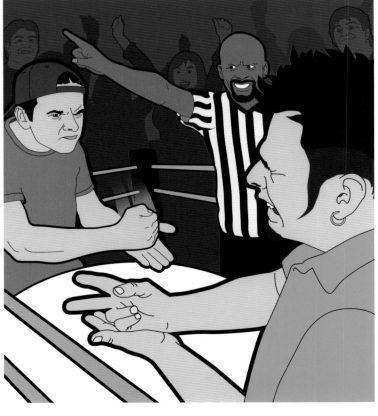

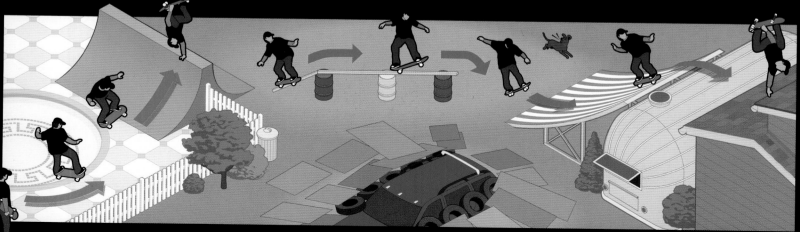

Anthony Rule

Anthony Rule Illustration
31 Whernside Road
Woodthorpe
Nottingham NG54LD
UK

☎ + 44 (0)1159 264 941
📱 + 44 (0)7767 656 653
✉ info@anthonyrule.co.uk
🌐 www.anthonyrule.co.uk
🌐 www.contact-me.net/AnthonyRule

Character development, children's books, advertising, greetings cards, caricature, packaging, board games, editorial, flash animation.
Full online portfolio.

Further samples available on request.

Recent clients include:
Tesco
Asda
Whsmith
Saatchi & Saatchi
Berol
OUP
Harcourt
BT
F1
and many more!

Russ Tudor

2 Hathaway Drive
Astley Bridge
Bolton BL1 7RY
UK

☎ + 44 (0)1204 597 795
✉ cartoons@russtudor.wanadoo.co.uk
🌐 www.russtudor.com
🌐 www.contact-me.net/RussTudor

Clients include: BBC, Royal Mail,
Disney, Euromoney, Empire, Maxim,
Evening Standard, Time Out, Radio
Times, The Economist, Media Week,
Financial World, Reed Healthcare,
Waitrose, IOD, British Airways,
Square Mile, The Scotsman,
The Times, The Sunday Times,
The Independent, Pentel, Halifax Bank,
Police Federation, Payroll World, Red,
Now, Runners World, Virgin.

Robin Edmonds

21 Boscobel Road North
St Leonards on Sea
East Sussex TN38 0NY
UK

☎ + 44 (0)1424 457 646
✉ rednoze@mac.com
🌐 www.robinedmonds.moonfruit.com
🌐 www.contact-me.net/RobinEdmonds

See also Contact 16–23

Colin Mier

21 Balmuir Gardens
Putney
London SW15 6NG
UK

☎ *+ 44 (0)20 8789 7556*
📱 *+ 44 (0)7050 153 929*
✉ *colin.mier@talk21.com*
🌐 *www.colinmier.com*
🌐 *www.contact-me.net/ColinMier*

Illustration and character/logo design
for advertising, editorial, print,
publishing and animation

Commissioned for UK and European
clients.

A comprehensive set of samples is
available on request.

Bryan Ceney

5 Corbiere Court
Thornton Road
Wimbledon
London SW19 4ND
UK

☎ + 44 (0)20 8947 2675
✉ bryan@bryanceney.co.uk
🌐 www. bryanceney.co.uk
🌐 www.contact-me.net/BryanCeney

Redseal

Début Art & The Coningsby Gallery
30 Tottenham Street
London W1T 4RJ
UK

☎ + 44 (0)20 7636 1064
☎ + 44 (0)20 7636 7478
📠 + 44 (0)20 7580 7017
📧 info@debutart.com
🌐 www.debutart.com

Redseal aim to create imaginative, stylish imagery using a combination of their own or client supplied photography and hand rendered and 3D elements.

Previous clients incl: Virgin, Orange, Mates, Cingular (USA), MacLaren F1, Ford, Clarke's Shoes, NASDAQ, 20th Century Fox, Microsoft, Harlequin (USA), BP, IBM, Xerox, SEAT Cars, Citibank, Random House (USA), Macmillan Books, .net Mag., Real Deals Mag., Televisual Mag., The Economist, Builder Mag., Computer Arts Mag.

Further examples of Redseal's work can be found in their extensive folio on-line at www.debutart.com

the coningsby gallery

Comm. by Redezine (USA) for The 50th Grammy Awards Program Book.

Comm. by Smartworks (Australia) for a Simply Music keyboard learning programme.

Comm. by Smartworks (Australia) for a Simply Music keyboard learning programme.

Comm. by Maxim Mag. (USA) for an article about US Prison Facilities.

Ian Mitchell

UK

☎ *+ 44 (0)116 270 8543*
📱 *+ 44 (0)7770 575 246*
✉ *inky.mitch@virgin.net*
🌐 *www.inkymitch.com*
🌐 *www.ianmitchellart.co.uk*
🌐 *www.contact-me.net/IanMitchell*

Illustration for editorial, advertising, publishing and design sectors.

Please contact me for further samples of work or view websites and previous Contact books.

Lemonade Illustration Agency

Hill House
Suite 231
210 Upper Richmond Road
London SW15 6NP
UK

☎ + 44 (0)7891 390 750
📧 info@lemonadeillustration.com
🌐 www.lemonadeillustration.com

Representing many leading
illustrators in all major areas
of the creative industry.

Please take a look at the new
sections on our website including:
Children's section
Motion
Storyboards
Corporate Identity

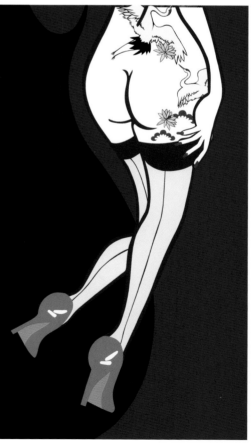

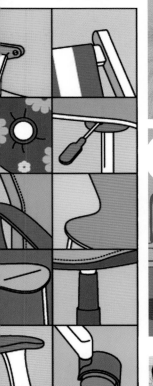

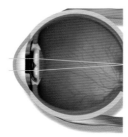
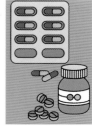
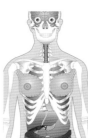
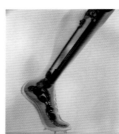
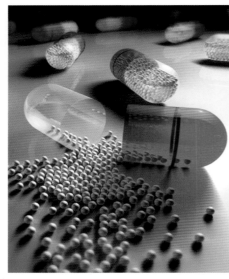

LEMONADE // STORYBOARDS

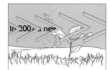

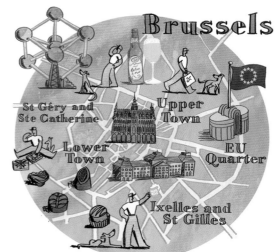

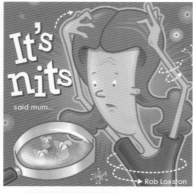

It's nits
said mum...
► Rob Loxston

Spooky Jelly Bats

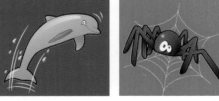

a is for apple   b is for bear   c is for caterpillar

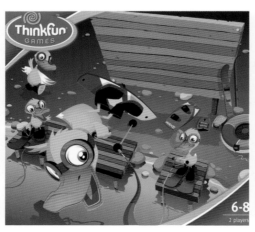

Gary Swift Studios

UK

☎ + 44 (0)1977 646 431
📱 + 44 (0)7967 554 595
✉ gary@garyswift.com
🌐 www.garyswift.com

*Many years experience working in
all media and in all creative sectors.
Check out my website for much more
and to see the animation section.*

Also represented by:
Lemonade Illustration Agency
🌐 *www.lemonadeillustration.com*

DON'T GET STUNG.
COME AND SEE OUR
NEW FIXED RATE
MORTGAGES...

Come on in
and see the
new interactive
channel

Gary Redford

London
UK

☎ + 44 (0)7903 584 937
✉ gary@garyredford.com
🌐 www.garyredford.com
🌐 www.contact-me.net/GaryRedford

Vector illustration for design, advertising, products and publishing including Oxford University Press, Kellogg's, Virgin Holidays.

See also online folio at
www.garyredford.com

Also represented by
Lemonade Illustration Agency

Comm. by Oxford University Press

Comm. by Kitcatt Nohr Alexander Shaw for Virgin Holidays

Eamon O'Donoghue

Southampton
UK

☎ + 44 (0)23 8071 0328
📱 + 44 (0)7729 482 562
✉ eamon@theextremist.co.uk
🌐 www.theextremist.co.uk
🌐 www.contact-me.net/EamonODonoghue

Eamon O'Donoghue offers the complete package from illustration straight through to print ready design. His aim is to give impact to illustration and design briefs with iconic results.

Specialising in DVD, book, album and comic book covers, Eamon is all about achieving the client's needs through traditional or digital illustrations.

Previous clients include:
Macmillan Publishing, Scholastic, Nissan, Entertainment Rights Plc., Jetix, BCI Eclipse, React Records, Image Comics, Contender Entertainment Group,
Harvest House Publishers.

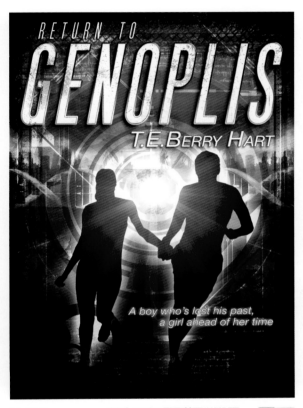

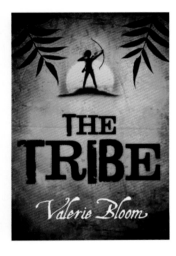

Andrew Holmes

19 Stamford Brook Avenue
Chiswick
London W6 0YB
UK

☎ + 44 (0)20 8741 9600
📱 + 44 (0)7803 257 792
✉ andy@andrewholmes.co.uk
🌐 www.andrewholmes.co.uk
🌐 www.contact-me.net/AndrewHolmes

Digital and conventional illustration.

Commissions for advertising, print, publishing & editorial, graphic art, design and film, architectural concepts, private and corporate artworks.

Please visit my site, call or email for more detailed information. Client list available on request.

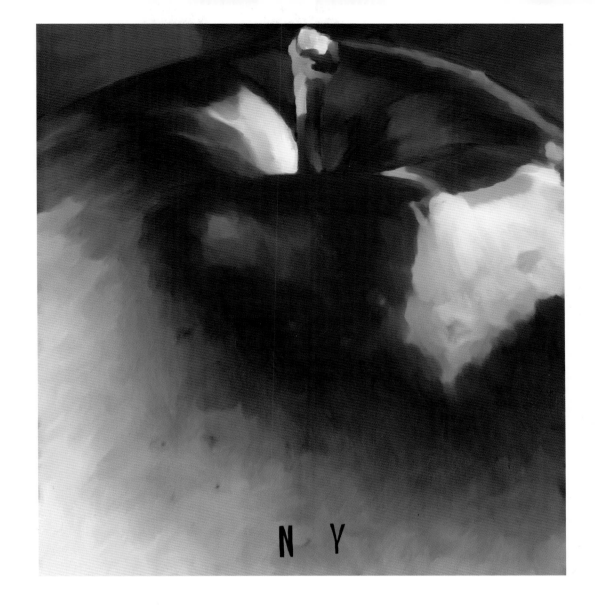

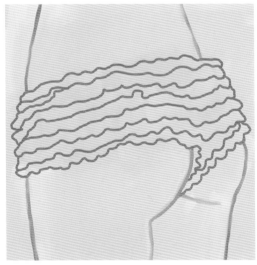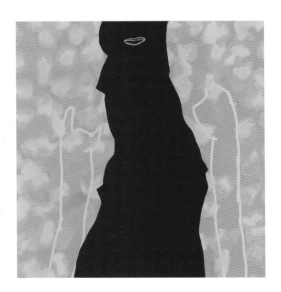

Andrew Holmes

Ⓜ + 44 (0)7803 257 792

Lesley Wakerley

iD2 Studio
Country House
Sea End Road
Benington
Lincolnshire PE22 0DQ
UK

T + 44 (0)1205 761 793
M + 44 (0)7799 673 153
E lesleywakerley@btinternet.com
W www.lesleywakerley.co.uk

Highly finished digital illustration for product packaging, advertising and publishing. Extensive website portfolio. Call or email Lesley to discuss your project.

Pat Thorne

19 Jubilee Terrace
Norwich
Norfolk NR1 2HT
UK

☎ + 44 (0)1603 614 845
📱 + 44 (0)7740 102 728
✉ patthorne@computekmail.co.uk
🌐 www.contact-me.net/PatThorne

Recent clients include:
Memac Ogilvy and Mather
Magnetic North
The World Health Organisation
Oxbridge

See Contacts 12, 13, 14 and 18.

Alex Williamson

Début Art & The Coningsby Gallery
30 Tottenham Street
London W1T 4RJ
UK

☎ + 44 (0)20 7636 1064
☎ + 44 (0)20 7636 7478
🖷 + 44 (0)20 7580 7017
✉ info@debutart.com
🌐 www.debutart.com

Alex's work is a blend of graphic and photographic elements, combining elements of drawing, printmaking and digital image making.

Previous clients include: Citibank, Sony, MTV, Halcrow Engineering, Molson Beer, Havana Club Rum, Phillip Morris, Inc., BBC Radio One, The Home Office, NatWest,

ICM Models, Penguin, Orion, Macmillan, Random House, HarperCollins, The Guardian, The Independent, Sunday Times, The FT, The Economist, Esquire, GQ,

More of Alex's work can be found in his extensive portfolio online at www.debutart.com

the coningsby gallery

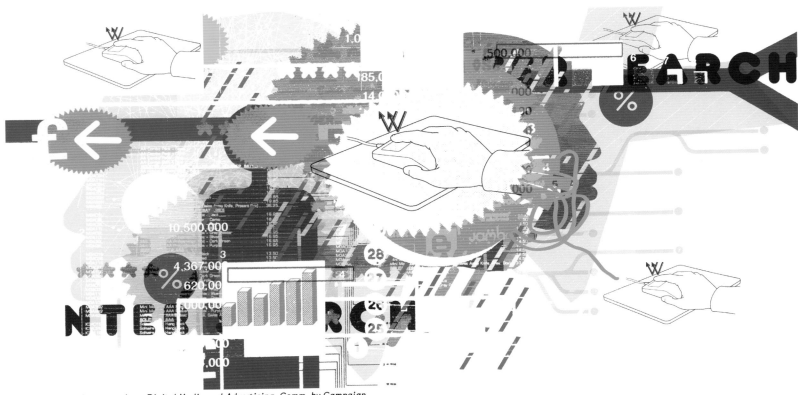

One of a series of images about Digital Media and Advertising. Comm. by Campaign.

Comm. by AOPA Magazine (USA) for article about Planes and Wildlife.

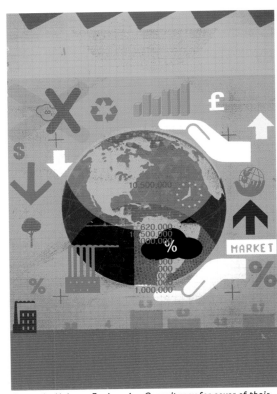

Comm. by Halcrow Engineering Consultancy for cover of their magazine 'Zeitgeist'.

Comm. by Farm for Lastminute.com

An ad for Citibank ad for use in The New Yorker.

Comm. by Hodder Books for cover of book 'Merton Brown'.

'European History and Culture', Comm. by The Chronicle.

Peter Crowther Associates

Début Art & The Coningsby Gallery
30 Tottenham Street
London W1T 4RJ
UK

☎ + 44 (0)20 7636 1064
☎ + 44 (0)20 7636 7478
📠 + 44 (0)20 7580 7017
✉ info@debutart.com
🌐 www.debutart.com

Peter Crowther Associates' digital image-making is widely regarded as representing a gold standard both technically and conceptually. They aim to produce photo-realistic images using the latest leading edge Maya Unlimited 3D software from Alias & Pixar's RenderMan. 3D models are created from scratch and rendered with custom shaders using feature film strength rendering from Pixar.

Previous clients incl: Camelot, P&O, AMEX, Allen & Gerritsen (USA), BP, BBDO (USA), Banco Di Roma, Virgin, Vodafone, Subaru, Smirnoff, Rolex, Prada, NEC, Entrepreneur Mag., The BBC, The Observer, C4, Publix, IBM, Lindt, NYSE, NASDAQ. More examples of their work can be found on pages 298-299 in Contact 23 and in their folio on the web at www.debutart.com

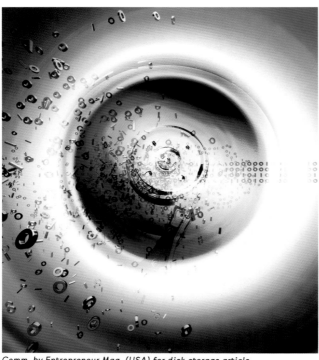

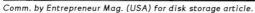

Comm. by Entrepreneur Mag. (USA) for disk storage article.

Comm. by New Scientist Mag. for vaccinations article.

Comm. by Findlay Publ. for MP3 functionality article.

Cover image for SM Magazine.

Comm. by Entrepreneur Mag (USA) for article about folding PDA's.

Comm. by The Central Office of Information (Home Office) for The RAF.

Comm. by Findlay Publ. for Machinery Magazine front cover.

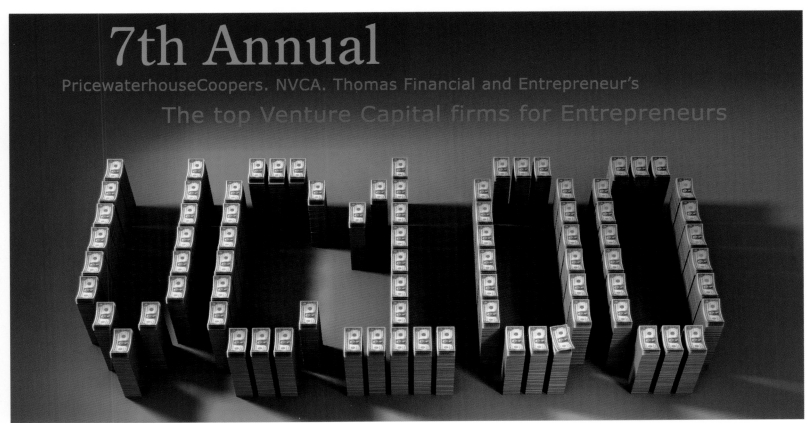

7th Annual

PricewaterhouseCoopers. NVCA. Thomas Financial and Entrepreneur's
The top Venture Capital firms for Entrepreneurs

Commissioned by Entrepreneur Magazine (USA) for front cover.

Flatliner V2

Début Art & The Coningsby Gallery
30 Tottenham Street
London W1T 4RJ
UK

☎ + 44 (0)20 7636 1064
☎ + 44 (0)20 7636 7478
🖷 + 44 (0)20 7580 7017
✉ info@debutart.com
🌐 www.debutart.com

FlatlinerV2 (aka Jason Jaroslav Cook) creates esoteric and highly contemporary images for clients attracted to his work worldwide. Combining 2D, 3D and photographic elements, FlatlinerV2 produces work for print, new media, TV broadcast and internet use.

Previous clients incl: Virgin, Westfield, Bloomingdales, BT, Miller Beer, Camel,

MTV, VH1, Motorola, The BeeGees, Barcardi, Ford (UK), The Economist, Marie Claire Mag., Time Out, NME, Toni & Guy, Men's Health Mag., HarperCollins Books, Nature Mag, The Guardian Guide, Focus Magazine, BA's Highlife Mag.

More of Flatliner V2's work can be found in his extensive portfolio on-line at www.debutart.com

Jay-Z & Reanna for The Grammy's 50th Annual Awards Program Book. Comm. by Rikki Poulos at Redezine.

Comm. for Bloomingdales by Brierley + Partners.

Comm. for a press and poster campaign for William Hill by Prego Ltd.

FIERCE ANGEL
PRESENTS
FIERCE DISCO II

Fierce Disco/Fierce Angels re-branding and illustration. Comm. by Fierce Angels Records.

Bargrooves CD covers. Comm. by Gary Baker at Loman Street Studios.

Camel Ashtrays. Comm. by Agent 16 (USA).

Paul Bateman

UK

☎ + 44 (0)1912 585 742
📱 + 44 (0)7980 344 406
📧 paul@paulbateman.co.uk
🌐 www.paulbateman.co.uk
🌐 www.contact-me.net/PaulBateman

I create collage & photomontage illustrations by manipulating found, original and given imagery for editorial, publishing and advertising clients.

Visit my website to see further examples of commissioned work, which utilise a variety of collage & montage techniques.

The Independent – Fool Britannia (Measuring the nation's intelligence)

Iain McIntosh

23 Fettes Row
Edinburgh
EH3 6RH
UK

T + 44 (0)131 5557 0211
E iain@iain-mac.com
W www.iain-mac.com
W www.contact-me.net/IainMcIntosh

My line illustrations feature on labels and packaging for leading brands from Glenmorangie Scotch whisky to Patak's Indian food.

I've drawn mastheads for several newspapers in Europe and Africa. Publishing work includes illustrated novels and bookjackets for best-selling author Alexander McCall Smith and I recently illustrated and designed 'The No.1 Ladies' Detective Agency Collectors' Edition'.

My work has appeared in award-winning packaging, publishing and advertising.

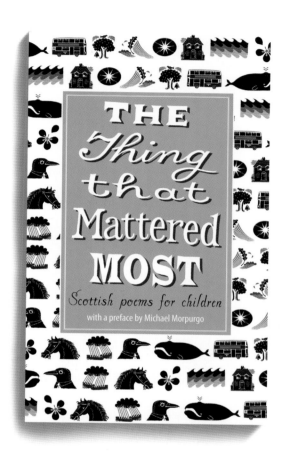

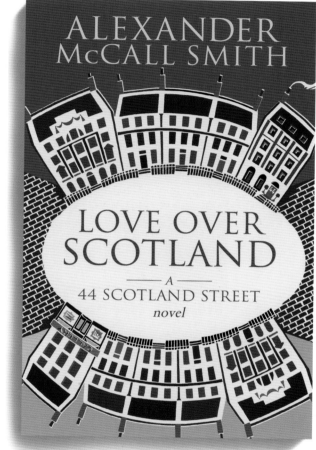

Rian Hughes

Device
2 Blake Mews
Kew Gardens
TW9 3GA
UK

☎ + 44 (0)20 8896 0626 (UK)
☎ 347 535 0626 (US Skype)
✉ rian@rianhughes.com
🌐 www.rianhughes.com
🌐 www.contact-me.net/RianHughes

Graphic illustration, illustrative graphics, typography, logo design. Type and image treated as an integrated whole.

Please check out the redesigned Device website, featuring: extensive updated portfolios covering illustration, logo design, graphic design and photography.

500+ Device fonts available for immediate download. Prints and merchandise. The Device message board... and download a free font!

See also past Contacts.

Robbie Polley

144 Southgate Road
London N1 3HX
UK

☎ + 44 (0)20 7254 0576
📠 + 44 (0)20 7684 1510
📱 + 44 (0)7973 248 745
✉ robbiepolley@blueyonder.co.uk
🌐 www.robbiepolley.co.uk
🌐 www.contact-me.net/RobbiePolley

I've specialised in architectural illustration since 1989. Primarily I visualise early conceptual ideas, capturing the spirit of a project. I use pencil, watercolour and line, I usually then edit and enhance in Photoshop. Alternatively I can work on detailed axonometric or aerial views with a high degree of detail and naturalism. I can be relied upon to complete within tight deadlines and budgets.

Image top; St Marks Square for the book "Venice in Peril".
Lower right; presentation visual for Terry Farrell Architects.
Lower left; Cut-away watercolour of The Royal Institute of Great Britain.

Rowena Dugdale

Début Art & The Coningsby Gallery
30 Tottenham Street
London W1T 4RJ
UK

☎ + 44 (0)20 7636 1064
☎ + 44 (0)20 7636 7478
🖷 + 44 (0)20 7580 7017
✉ info@debutart.com
🖥 www.debutart.com

Rowena creates her distinctive illustration style using a highly individual combination of darkroom photographic, digital and mixed media processes.

Previous clients include: The American Association for the Advancement of Science, The Institute of Directors, BBC Worldwide, Scottish Enterprise, Summertime Publishing, Future Publishing, Newhall Publishing, Reed Business Information, Candis Mag., Community Care Mag.,

Further examples of Rowena's work can be found on pages 214–215 in Contact 20 and in her folio on the web at www.debutart.com

the coningsby gallery

'Tiger.' One of 12 Chinese Zodiacs for Spirit & Destiny Mag.

'Wildsong.' Comm. BBC Wildlife Mag.

'Depression & Prozac.' Comm. by New Scientist Mag.

'Scrapbook.' Book Jacket. Comm. by Quarto Publ.

Andy Peters

Norwich
UK

M + 44 (0)7759 296 237
E andy@andypeters.net
W www.andypeters.net
W www.contact-me.net/AndyPeters

Caroline Jayne Church

Studio
100c West Street
Farnham
Surrey GU9 7EN
UK

T + 44 (0)1252 820 036
M + 44 (0)7932 605 855
E carolinesline@btconnect.com
W www.carolinejaynechurch.com
W www.contact-me.net/CarolineJayneChurch

Award winning illustrator with many years experience in advertising, packaging, character creation, paper products and children's publishing.

Substantial client list. Please visit my website for more information.

Caroline Jayne Church

M + 44 (0)7932 605 855

Kerry Roper

Début Art & The Coningsby Gallery
30 Tottenham Street
London W1T 4RJ
UK

☎ + 44 (0)20 7636 1064
☎ + 44 (0)20 7636 7478
📠 + 44 (0)20 7580 7017
✉ info@debutart.com
🌐 www.debutart.com

Kerry's work is known across the globe. It combines traditional illustration, photography and typography. He has exhibited at the Native Weapon exhibition 2004, the a.k.a. Gallery in Rome 2005 and 4walls in 2006. His work has appeared in many books and magazines including 'It's a Matter of Illustration' by Victionary, 'Thousand Type Treatments' by Rockport, 'Typographics' by Rotovision and a major feature in the Japanese design magazine '+81'.

Previous clients incl: Nike, Snickers, MacUser Mag., Digit Mag., Hed Kandi Records, Peacefrog Records, Defected Records, New Scientist Mag., Arena Mag., Computer Arts Mag.

www.debutart for full online portfolio.

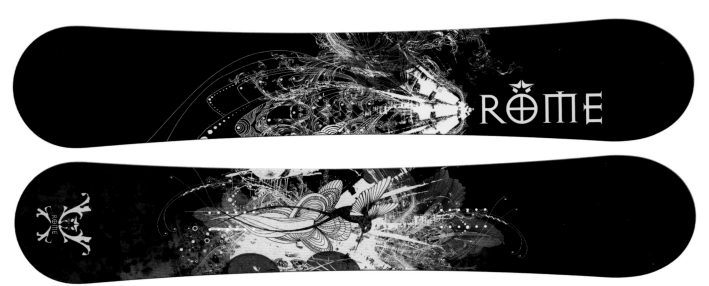

Snow boards. Comm. by Rome.

'Dolled Up To The Nines'. Photography by Cameron Krone.

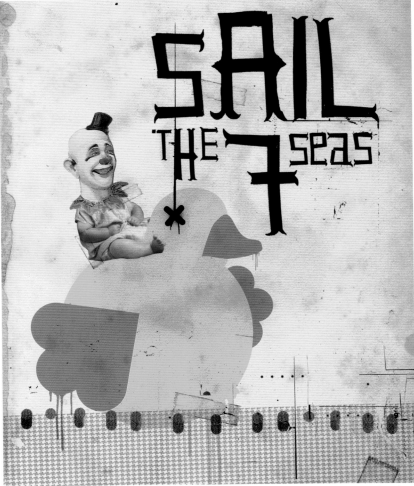

'Sail the Seven Seas'. Part of the 'If You Could Do Anything' project.

Fashion feature image. Comm. by Men's Health Mag. (Germany).

'Rex'. Part of the Designersblock Illustrate Exhibition 2007.

Self-initiated.

Comm. by MCBD Adv. for Subaru Cars.

Sim Marriott

UK

☎ + 44 (0)1726 67 101
📱 + 44 (0)7929 865 338
✉ sim@simmarriott.com
🌐 www.simmarriott.com
🌐 www.contact-me.net/SimMarriott

Dave Franks Illustration

Magenta House
21 Horace Road
Barkingside, Ilford
Essex IG6 2BG
UK

T + 44 (0)20 8551 2054
M + 44 (0)7949 969 351
E on request
W www.davefranks.com
W www.contact-me.net/DaveFranks

Comm. by
Turnbull Grey
'London Prepared'
Poster Series

Comm. American Halloween
Client: The Cuckoo Club

6' Hero-figures
under licence to
Dell Computers

(below) Comm. by
Grey Advertising
for Pharmaceutical
Ad Campaign

Comm. by CEO of

(above) Comm. for Syngenta Ad Campaign Series

EEK!...
I USED TO FEEL SAFE WALKING ALONE, BUT NOT ANYMORE...

...TRY AS HE MIGHT THERE SEEMED NO WAY OUT OF THE RUT FOR YOUNG JASON...

..WHAT THE!

..ONE DAY THE **SPIRIT MASTER OF YDACHI** PAID JASON A VISIT... ONE THAT WOULD CHANGE HIS LIFE FOR EVER..NOW HE COULD LEAVE THE STREET LIFE BEHIND AND DISCOVER HIS TRUE POTENTIAL...

Leo Broadley

81 Princes Avenue
Walsall
West Midlands WS1 2DG
UK

☎ + 44 (0)1922 624 992
📱 + 44 (0)7779 465 122
✉ broadley@madasafish.com
🌐 www.contact-me.net/LeoBroadley

Illustration for work in publishing, advertising and design.

Clients include:

Ernest and Julio Gallo Winery
American International Group
Elvis Communications
Juice Relationship Marketing

Scholastic Children's Books
Meadowside Children's Books
Oxford University Press
Michael O'Mara Books
Franklin Watts

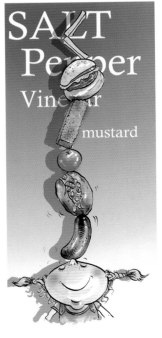

Peter Mac

UK

T + 44 (0)1273 706 914
M + 44 (0)7734 593 448
E peter@brighton.co.uk
W www.peter-mac.com
W aoiportfolios.com/artist/petermac
W www.contact-me.net/PeterMac

Short

Kingfisher Business Centre
Burnley Road
Rawtenstall
Rossendale
Lancashire BB4 8EQ
UK

☎ + 44 (0)1706 836 050
📱 + 44 (0)7786 167 030
✉ enquiries@short-cgi.com
🌐 www.short-cgi.com

Short is a company who specialise in 3D/2D visualisation/illustration & animation for all types of industries such as Architectural, Engineering and Product design. Short's creative team have over 10 years experience in high end visualisation/illustration. Our aim is to provide our clients with artwork for advertising, training & marketing that exceed their expectation.

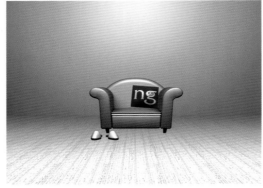

Gouty Foot

UK

T + 44 (0)1730 893 046
M + 44 (0)7901 582 677
E gary@goutyfoot.com
W www.goutyfoot.com
W www.contact-me.net/GoutyFoot

*Illustration, Character Design
& Development, Flash Animation
for web & TV.*

Come visit the ancestral website:
www.goutyfoot.com

See also:
Contacts 15–23

CN Images & Monkeys © Pesky

Magictorch

Studio 8
Level 5 South
New England House
New England Street
Brighton BN1 4GH
UK

☎ + 44 (0)1273 620 222
✉ info@magictorch.com
🌐 www.magictorch.com
🌐 www.contact-me.net/Magictorch

Magictorch creates digital illustrations covering a range of styles from flat vector graphics to highly polished 3D compositions and everything else in between.

Clients include: New Scientist, Computer Arts, Nokia, Catskills Records, Classic Rock, T3, Cingular.

Visit Magictorch.com to see our regularly updated online portfolio.

Anne Wilson

Illustration Ltd
2 Brooks Court
Cringle Street
London SW8 5BX
UK

T + 44 (0)20 7720 5202
F + 44 (0)20 7720 5920
E team@illustrationweb.com
W www.mywholeportfolio.com/AnneWilson
W www.contact-me.net/AnneWilson

Representatives in: USA, France, Deutschland & Singapore.

My hi-resolution portfolio is now available to print from the internet for your immediate presentation.

Illustration

Sobek
Crocodile

Climb aboard the river boat! We're sailing down the Nile.

We'll see the Cairo skyline in just a little while.

Arlene Adams

61 Oxford Road
Moseley
Birmingham B13 9ES
UK

T/F + 44 (0)1214 496 190
M + 44 (0)7833 682 916
E mail@arleneadams.com
W www.arleneadams.com
W www.contact-me.net/ArleneAdams

Uwe Mayer

31 Brandram's Wharf
127–131 Rotherhithe Street
London SE16 4NF
UK

☎ + 44 (0)7968 941 144
✉ illustration@uwemayer.com
🌐 www.uwemayer.com
🌐 www.contact-me.net/UweMayer

Lively illustration – from advertising to children's books.

For watercolour based work see also Contact 20, page 343.

Please visit my online-portfolio on www.uwemayer.com

Recent clients include:

McCann Erickson Europe, Bloomsbury, Usborne Publishing, Heinemann, Oxford University Press, Meadowside, Berlin Verlag, Rowohlt, Hallmark, Carlton Cards, Archant Dialogue, Nestlé.

Peter Richardson

7 Bowman's Drive
Battle
East Sussex TN33 OLT
UK

☎ + 44 (0)1424 774 170
📠 + 44 (0)1424 775 331
✉ p-r@dircon.co.uk
🌐 peter-richardson-illustration.moonfruit.com
🌐 www.contact-me.net/PeterRichardson

Having freed himself from the chains of Mordus and escaping from the Planet Xeron the premier illustrator otherwise known as Galactacus has journeyed to planet Earth and is available for a very limited time only to attend to your illustration requirements.

Nominated for the Kate Greenaway Award 2008 for illustrations to the Boffin Boy series of books published by Ransom Books – check website for further details.

James Ineson

15 Wilton Grove
Headingley
Leeds LS6 4ES
UK

T + 44 (0)113 3792 508
M + 44 (0)7961 574 662
E james@skry.co.uk
E contact@skry.co.uk
W www.skry.co.uk
W www.contact-me.net/JamesIneson

James Ineson is a neo traditionalist illustrator with over 14 years experience in hand painted historical styles. He attracts clients worldwide.

All his artwork is completely original, observing the styles, techniques and the largely forgotten rules pioneered by the patternbook masters.

The painted work is supplied in a scanned format which will be further digitally engineered to repeat easily if necessary.

Genny Haines

UK

Children's publishing, greeting cards,
packaging, editorial, stationery,
advertising.

Please phone for samples.
List of clients on my website.

T + 44 (0)1252 717 444
M + 44 (0)7969 849 832
E gennyhaines@btinternet.com
W www.contact-me.net/GennyHaines

Jamie Sneddon

Brighton
UK

☎ + 44 (0)1273 67 22 11
📱 + 44 (0)7779 71 53 53
✉ jamie@jamiesneddon.co.uk
🌐 www.jamiesneddon.co.uk
🌐 www.contact-me.net/JamieSneddon

Recently commissioned by Alan Burrows Ltd, on behalf of Mazda. Jamie Sneddon was briefed to illustrate 10 full feature spreads for Mazda's Pan-European brochure, launching the new Mazda 6. Over the following 4 pages, 2 of these spreads are presented amongst other works. To see the other Mazda pieces along with many more samples please visit my websites, as well as Contacts 18–23, or portfolio by request. Other clients include: KIA Motors [c/o David & Goliath, LA], Lexus, BMW, Toyota, Carre Noir, Beechwood, The Guardian, Daily Telegraph, Ministry of Sound, Codemasters, O2, Virgin, Maxim (UK, USA & Internationals), Esquire, Men's Health, Official PSP mag, Official Xbox 360 mag, Time Out, Blender, XXL, Spin, Dennis Pub, Nat Mags, Emap, Condé Nast & Future publishing.

Mazda 6 brochure cover [environment only, all vehicles were studio shot]: Comm by Alan Burrows Ltd

PS3 to PSP away from home wifi connectivity: Comm by Official PSP magazine

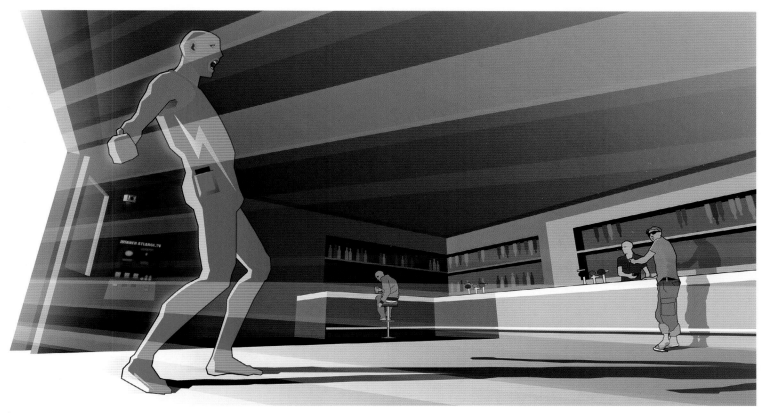

Pink Spandex

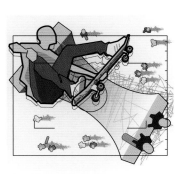

Skate filming techniques: Comm by Maxim US

Jamie Sneddon **T** + 44 (0)1273 67 22 11 **M** + 44 (0)7779 71 53 53

Mazda 6 brochure spread
[environment only, all vehicles were studio shot]:
Comm by Alan Burrows Ltd

"Re-animating" old skool game characters: Comm by Official PSP magazine

Self defense: Comm by Maxim US

Jamie Sneddon ☎ + 44 (0)1273 67 22 11 Ⓜ + 44 (0)7779 71 53 53

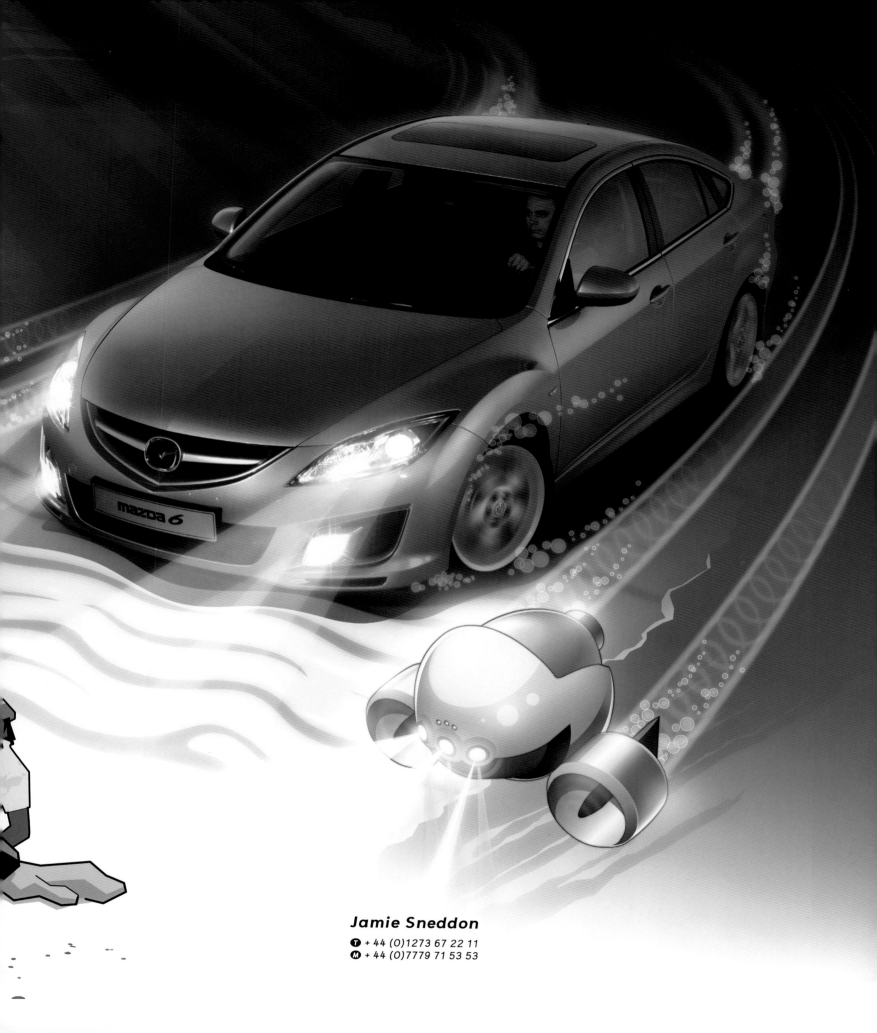

Jamie Sneddon

+ 44 (0)1273 67 22 11
+ 44 (0)7779 71 53 53

Gary Newman

London
UK

☎ + 44 (0)7903 584 937
✉ gary@garynewman.co.uk
🌐 www.garynewman.co.uk

Digital illustration for clients worldwide, including BBC, Debenhams, Gillette, Kellogg's, Mattel, Sony, Virgin.

Extensive portfolio online at:
www.garynewman.co.uk

See also Contact 23 pages 20–21
Contact 22 page 288
Contact 21 page 173
Also represented by Lemonade.

Comm. by Debenhams

Part of an 85 metre long panel. Comm. by Greater Manchester Passenger Transport Authority.

Comm. by Kellogg's

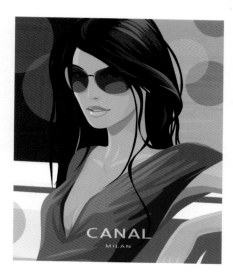

CANAL
MILAN

Comm. by Mattel (USA) 3 of over 40 figures of Barbie. The image of Barbie® is the property of Mattel, Inc. and may not be reproduced without express written permission.

Comm. by Red Cell (Paris) for Marques Avenue

The Organisation

UK Office

New York Office

Pauline Mason

☎ 0845 054 8033 (UK only)
☎ + 44 (0)20 7833 8268
📠 + 44 (0)20 7833 8269
📱 + 44 (0)7973 172 902
✉ info@organisart.co.uk
🌐 www.organisart.co.uk
🌐 www.contact-me.net/TheOrganisation

☎ + 1 917 586 6514
✉ masonpmac@yahoo.com

*Over 70 portfolios online –
Cutting edge international image
makers.
Search by
Style – Medium – Subject Matter
Large Stock Library online –
Easy solutions to impossible deadlines
Purchase your favourite artwork –
www.illustrationgallery.co.uk*

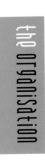

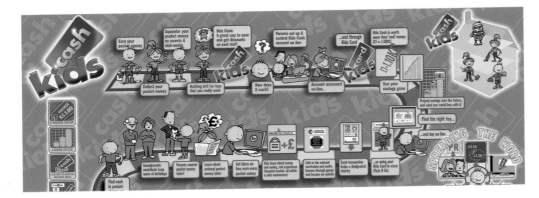

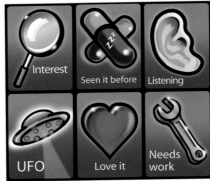

Three keys Processes

Ongoing creative brief
and creative work guidance

Management of
Regional Projects

Harnessing the creative
resources of the Network

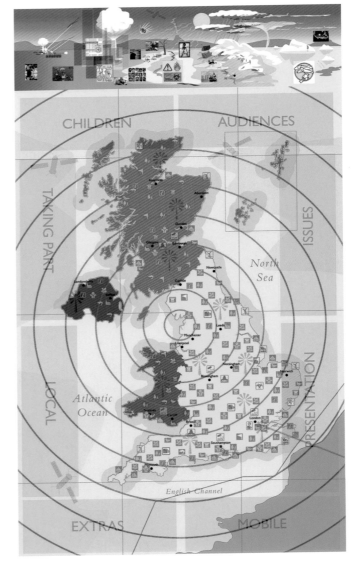

Steve Dell

Richard Merritt

Lynn Heaton

4 Old School Close
Alweston
Sherborne
Dorset DT9 5HT
UK

T + 44 (0)1963 235 94
M + 44 (0)7796 965 757
E lynn@lynnheaton.com
W www.lynnheaton.com
W www.contact-me.net/LynnHeaton

Clients include a variety of children's book publishers including Walker Books and also many of the leading greeting card companies.

Amanda Enright

96 Royal George Road
Burgess Hill
West Sussex
RH15 9SL
UK

T + 44 (0)1444 870 878
M + 44 (0)7947 469 769
E amanda.enright@btopenworld.com
W www.contact-me.net/AmandaEnright

Duck Egg Blue

100 Bowbridge Gardens
Bottesford
Nottinghamshire NG13 0AZ
UK

☎ + 44 (0)1949 845 176
✉ info@duckeggbluedesign.com
🌐 www.duckeggbluedesign.com
🌐 www.contact-me.net/DuckEggBlue

Duck Egg Blue is a small illustration and design team, who thrive on creating fresh and lively designs for children's books, games and packaging.

For an informal chat about how we might be able to help you, please do get in touch.

Some of our recent clients include:

Kingfisher Publications
Early Learning Centre
Clementoni SpA
Igloo Books
Award Publications
Gibsons Games
Mothercare

duckeggblue

After a busy day, the animals are tired. The sun goes down and the moon and stars appear.

Yawn! It's time to go to sleep.

"I'm going to sleep in the tree!"

"I'm going to count the stars!"

"Goodnight!" says the biggest animal.

"Goodnight!" squeak the smallest animals.

Zzzz!

Alexander Beeching

UK

T *+ 44 (0)1242 227 696*
E *beechingalexbeeching@hotmail.com*
W *www.inkandar.com*
W *www.contact-me.net/AlexanderBeeching*

Watercolour, digital, hand-drawn with pen and ink
Commissioned by Beechwood.

Watercolour, digital, photomontage, hand-drawn with
pen and ink
Self-commissioned

Pencil, digital and watercolour
Self-commissioned.

Martin Fish

UK

M + 44 (0)7790 241 522
E martin@martinfishart.com
W www.martinfishart.com
W www.contact-me.net/MartinFish

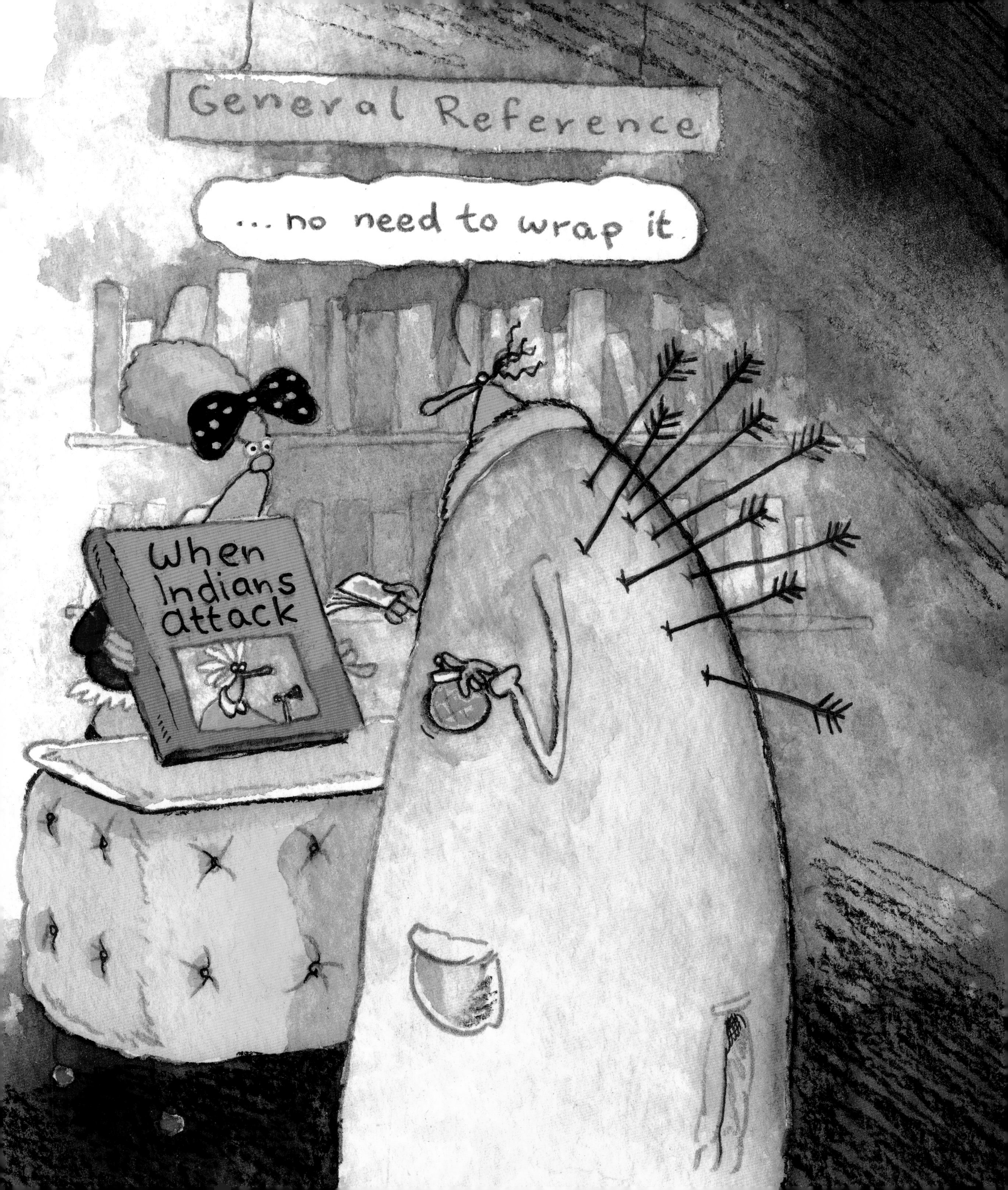
General Reference
... no need to wrap it.
When Indians attack

Steven Pattison

Illustration Ltd
2 Brooks Court
Cringle Street
London SW8 5BX
UK

T *+ 44 (0)20 7720 5202*
F *+ 44 (0)20 7720 5920*
E *team@illustrationweb.com*
W *www.mywholeportfolio.com/StevenPattison*
W *www.contact-me.net/StevenPattison*

Representatives in: USA, France, Deutschland & Singapore.

My hi-resolution portfolio is now available to print from the internet for your immediate presentation.

Sally Kindberg

126a Gloucester Avenue
London NW1 8JA
UK

📞 + 44 (0)20 7722 6600
📱 + 44 (0)7810 455 552
✉ k@sallykindberg.co.uk
🌐 www.sallykindberg.co.uk
🌐 www.contact-me.net/SallyKindberg

Clients include:

Bloomsbury Children's Books
The Independent
English Heritage
Barnes & Noble
The Guardian

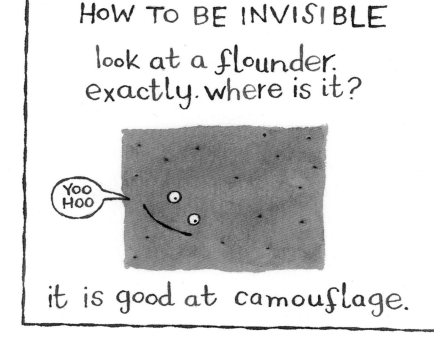

Tony Sigley

210 St Peter's Street
Lowestoft NR32 2LZ
UK

T + 44 (0)1502 515 984
M + 44 (0)7816 419 097
E tonysigley@madasafish.com
W www.contact-me.net/TonySigley

Illustration for print, publishing, advertising and editorial.
Over 10 years scratching, scribbling and etching out a living in advanced finger-painting. In this time I have developed a range of styles and honed my skills in both hand-drawn and digital illustration.
To look at the bigger picture, contact me for samples.

Clients Include:
Oxford University Press, Future Publishing, Origin Publishing, James Pembroke Publishing, Specialist Publications, Redwood Publishing, The Big Issue, Calpol, Camelot, The Co-operative, Harrods, NPower, Peugeot, Saga, Sage, The Schools Council, Specsavers, Teacher Training Agency...

TONY SIGLEY
ILLUSTRATOR

Penny Sobr

132 Catharine Street
Cambridge CB1 3AR
UK

T + 44 (0)7814 807 723
E penny@pennysobr.com
W www.pennysobr.com
W www.contact-me.net/PennySobr

Agent:

Lemonade Illustration
London
UK

T + 44 (0)7891 390 750

Clientèle include:
You Magazine, Glamour Magazine,
Penguin Publishing,
Kensington Publishing,
Orion Publishing, WHSmith, Boots,
Saga Magazine, Swanky Modes brand,
Luscious Girls brand, Lagoon Group,
Creatively Different, Kandibox,
Superdrug, City & Guilds, NHS,
The Forster Group, Wilkinson & Sword,
Hilton Hotel, Tesco, IPC Magazines...

Ian Naylor

Illustration Ltd
2 Brooks Court
Cringle Street
London SW8 5BX
UK

☎ + 44 (0)20 7720 5202
📠 + 44 (0)20 7720 5920
✉ team@illustrationweb.com
🌐 www.mywholeportfolio.com/IanNaylor
🌐 www.contact-me.net/IanNaylor

Representatives in: USA, France,
Deutschland & Singapore.

My hi-resolution portfolio is now
available to print from the internet
for your immediate presentation.

Illustration

Karen Donnelly

94 Southover Street
Brighton BN2 9UD
UK

☎ + 44 (0)1273 673 747
✉ donnelly@brighton.co.uk
🅦 www.karendonnelly.com
🅦 www.contact-me.net/KarenDonnelly

David Semple

13 East Mount Road
York YO24 1BD
UK

T + 44 (0)1904 632 337
E drsemple@btopenworld.com
W www.davidsemple.co.uk
W www.contact-me.net/DavidSemple

Jacques Fabre

NB Illustration
40 Bowling Green Lane
Clerkenwell, London EC1R ONE
UK

☎ + 44 (0)20 7278 9131
📠 + 44 (0)20 7278 9121
✉ info@nbillustration.co.uk
🌐 www.nbillustration.co.uk
🌐 www.contact-me.net/JacquesFabre

Jacques Fabre works extensively in the packaging industry creating photo reaslistic imagery for clients worldwide including, Nestlé, Purina, Waitrose, United Biscuits, Cadbury's, Lindt, Materne, Affligem, Bonne Maman and many more. Jacques also creates realistic animal images for children's publishing and more recently the re-branding of Felix Cat foods.

Laurence Whiteley

NB Illustration
40 Bowling Green Lane
Clerkenwell, London EC1R 0NE
UK

T *+ 44 (0)20 7278 9131*
F *+ 44 (0)20 7278 9121*
E *info@nbillustration.co.uk*
W *www.nbillustration.co.uk*
W *www.contact-me.net/LaurenceWhiteley*

NB Illustration

NB Illustration
40 Bowling Green Lane
Clerkenwell, London EC1R 0NE
UK

T + 44 (0)20 7278 9131
F + 44 (0)20 7278 9121
E info@nbillustration.co.uk
W www.nbillustration.co.uk
W www.contact-me.net/NBIllustration

Our agency represents some of the finest commercial illustrators to the creative industry world-wide.

Featured artists:
Left page top: Ben Hasler
Left page bottom: Judy Stevens
Right page top: Sarah Nayler
Right page bottom: Jo Goodberry

NB Illustration
40 Bowling Green Lane
Clerkenwell, London EC1R 0NE
UK

Digital Progression

1st Floor
123 Old Christchurch Road
Bournemouth
BH1 1EP
UK

T + 44 (0)1202 316 660
F + 44 (0)1202 311 185
E mail@digitalprogression.com
W www.digitalprogression.com
W www.contact-me.net/DigitalProgression

Digital Progression is a UK studio specialising in high end digital artwork and graphics production for the advertising, design and games industries.

An in-house team of highly experienced artists, we offer the complete solution for digital image creation.

Recent clients include: Abbey, Barclays, BP, BSkyB, Bryant, Bupa, Clarks, Crest Nicholson, Direct Line, Ebay, Eidos, Electronic Arts, Emap, Filofax, The Football Association, GemsTV, Godrej, Hutchison 3G, Ikea, Kraft Foods, Liverpool Victoria, Lucasfilm, Mars, O2, PC World, Persimmons, Pioneer, Reuters, Sainsbury's, Taylor Woodrow, Xerox.

John See Illustration

34 Charterhouse Road
Godalming
Surrey GU7 2AQ
UK

T + 44 (0)1483 429 240
E john@see-illustration.com
E info@see-illustration.com
W www.see-illustration.com
W www.contact-me.net/JohnSee

Clean, clear and legible digital line illustration produced through 25 years experience.
To view my extensive portfolio or to request a set of colour sample cards, please visit my website.

Recent clients include:
Johnny Walker Whisky
Halifax Bank
Visa

Lee Cooper Jeans
Top Shop
Canary Wharf Developments
Ministry of Transport
BP Petrochemicals
Dunlop
Unilever
Marks & Spencer
Jack Daniels
The Economist

see

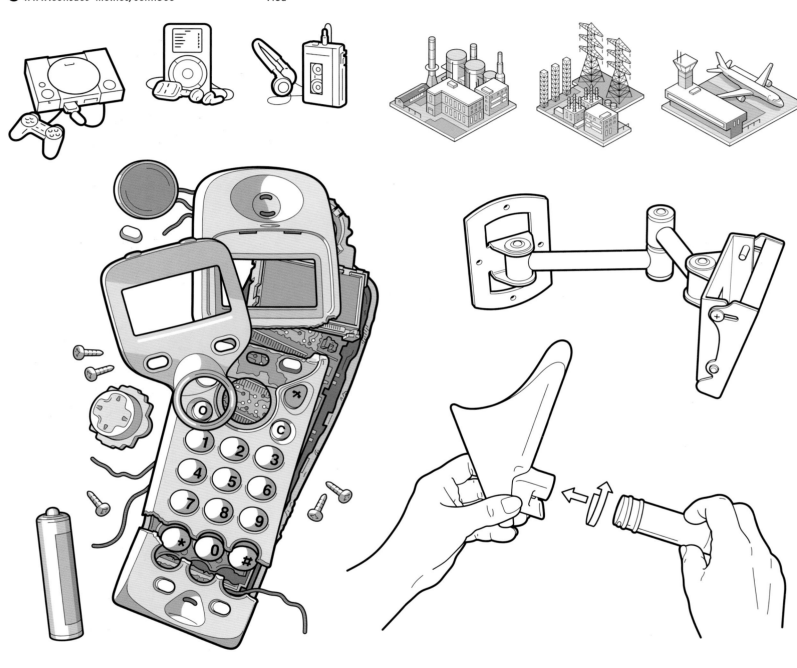

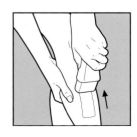
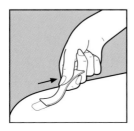

Bill Greenhead

Illustration Ltd
2 Brooks Court
Cringle Street
London SW8 5BX
UK

T + 44 (0)20 7720 5202
F + 44 (0)20 7720 5920
E team@illustrationweb.com
W www.mywholeportfolio.com/BillGreenhead
W www.contact-me.net/BillGreenhead

Representatives in: USA, France,
Deutschland & Singapore.

*My hi-resolution portfolio is now
available to print from the internet
for your immediate presentation.*

Illustration

345

John Batten

51 Stondon Park
London SE23 1LB
UK

☎ + 44 (0)20 8291 3365
📱 + 44 (0)7713 634 608
✉ jp.batten@btopenworld.com
🌐 www.JohnBatten.net
🌐 www.contact-me.net/JohnBatten

Versatile & experienced illustrator working digitally for print or web.

Recent clients include:
BT, Goldman Sachs,
Times Educational Supplement,
Prospect Magazine,
Oxford University Press,
Cambridge University Press,
Cornelsen, Public Finance,
Save The Children.

Please visit my website or see previous editions of Contact for more examples of my work.

John Batten

☎ + 44 (0)20 8291 3365

Inge-Marie Jensen

London
UK

☎ + 44 (0)20 8902 2529
📱 + 44 (0)7740 645 026
✉ inge.m.jensen@gmail.com
🌐 www.contact-me.net/Inge-MarieJensen

*Illustration for Advertising, Editorial,
Publishing and Design.*

See also:
Contact New Talent 2002 – page 64
Contact 22 – page 199
Contact 23 – page 302

*My clients appreciate a variety
of different styles which can be
viewed at:
www.contact-me/Inge-MarieJensen,
and range from figurative drawing to
a more stylised graphic interpretation
of their brief.*

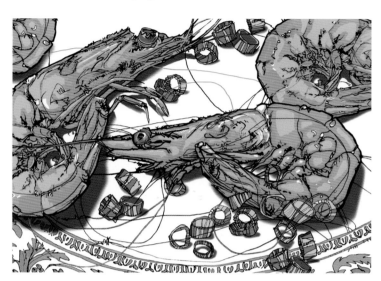

Sean Longcroft

Unit 8 Level 5 South
New England House
New England Street
Brighton BN1 4GH
UK

T + 44 (0)1273 623 808
F + 44 (0)1273 620 222
M + 44 (0)7967 349 037
E sean@longcroft.net
W www.longcroft.net

Gary Neill

UK

☎ + 44 (0)7973 866 739
🌐 www.garyneill.com

Over twelve years experience of creating strong, simple, playful ideas that are illustrated in a vibrant, graphic manner.

Visit www.garyneill.com

View Contact 11– 24

Call to see a portfolio

Lifesaving medication

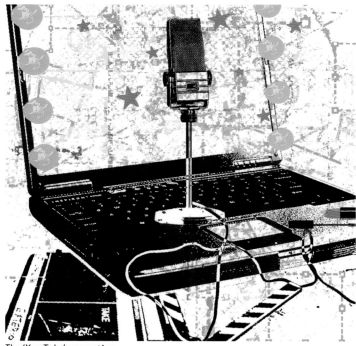

The 'You Tube' generation

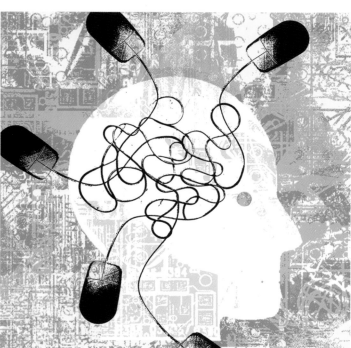

Online collaboration

Modern Rugby League

America in Iraq

Skiing accidents

Unbalanced portfolio

Investment risk

The Design Corporation

Ground Floor
7 Portland Mews
Soho
London W1F 8JQ
UK

T + 44 (0)20 7734 5676
M + 44 (0)7974 144 830
E us@designcorporation.co.uk
W www.design4music.com
W www.designcorporation.co.uk

The Design Corporation is a group of creatives offering a diverse style of digital illustration – Vector, 3D, photo realistc and typographic illustration. Within all these skills we offer contemporary and stylish images working across retail, the music industry and international media.

Services include: Digital illustration, 3D illustration, graphic design, web design, branding, photo retouching and image manipulation.

Clients include: EMI, Virgin, Universal, Disney, Sony BMG, Warner, Ministry Of Sound, The Arcadia Group, Polo Ralph Lauren, Marks & Spencer, Union Square, Vodafone.

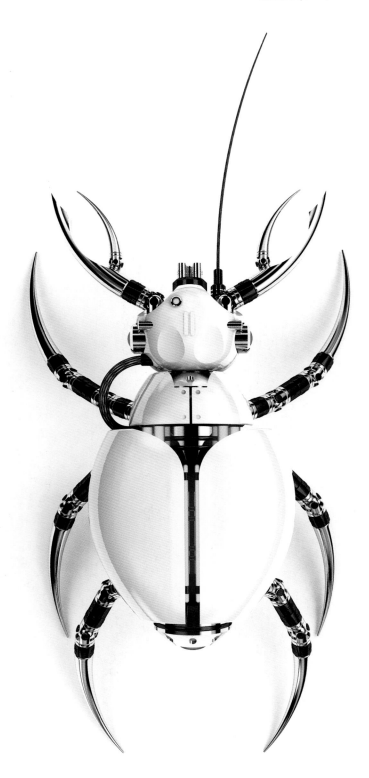

Coleoptera Robotus BEETLEBOT Mk.1

The Long & the Short of it

Bedfordshire
UK

☎ + 44 (0)1582 477 703
✉ jamesholderness@btconnect.com
🌐 www.contact-me.net/TheLongandtheShortofit

See more examples in Contact
15 (p.240), 16 (p.570),
17 (p.501), 18 (p.535),
19 (p.454), 20 (p.428),
21 (p.179), 22 (p.362–3)
and 23 (p.344–5) or give us a call.

Simon Clare Creative Workshop Ltd

Little Leydens, Stick Hill
Hartfield Road
Edenbridge
Kent TN8 5NH
UK

T + 44 (0)1732 862 672
E simonc.creative@btinternet.com
W www.contact-me.net/SimonClare

Tim Marrs

UK

T + 44 (0)7714 062 447
E tim@timmarrs.co.uk
W www.timmarrs.co.uk
W www.contact-me.net/TimMarrs

The illustrations shown include commissions for Automobile Magazine, Entertainment Weekly and Sol Beer, page 1 and page 2 includes Nike Asia, Weiden & Kennedy, Japan. Quicksilver Europe, T Shirt Design and Royal Palaces for ST&MP.

Clients include: Pepsi, Brand Jordan, Reebok, Kswiss, Nike, Geffen Records, EMI records, Ogilvy and Mather, Saatchi and Saatchi, Weiden & Kennedy, Publicis & Hal Riney, Orion Publishing, Random House Publishing, New Scientist Magazine, Reader's Digest, Mojo Magazine, BBC Active, Royal Mail, Big Issue, Entertainment Weekly, Estates Gazette and many more.

See also Contact:
17, 18, 19, 20, 22, 23

The Apple Agency Ltd

Design House
Exmoor Avenue
Scunthorpe
North Lincolnshire DN15 8NJ
UK

T + 44 (0)1724 289 081
F + 44 (0)1724 289 381
E info@apple.co.uk
W www.apple.co.uk
W www.contact-me.net/AppleAgency

Over 20 years production of "Traditional" and "Digital" illustration from over 150 artists and now including "3D Animation". Should you not find what you are looking for on www.apple.co.uk, then contact us and we will email additional samples from our image bank.

All artists are familiar with the latest technologies for image transfer, speeding up the process of supplying bespoke illustration.

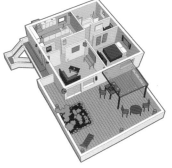

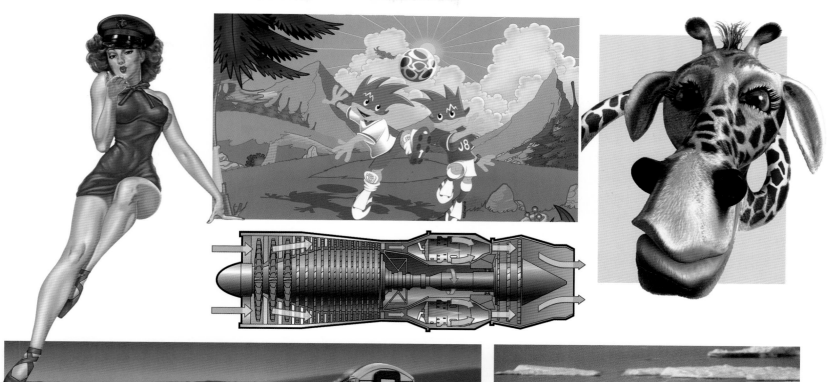
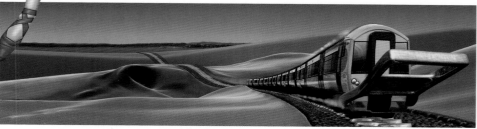

The Apple Agency Ltd

Design House
Exmoor Avenue
Scunthorpe
North Lincolnshire DN15 8NJ
UK

T + 44 (0)1724 289 081
F + 44 (0)1724 289 381
E info@apple.co.uk
W www.apple.co.uk
W www.contact-me.net/AppleAgency

Over 20 years production of "Traditional" and "Digital" illustration from over 150 artists and now including "3D Animation". Should you not find what you are looking for on www.apple.co.uk, then contact us and we will email additional samples from our image bank.

All artists are familiar with the latest technologies for image transfer, speeding up the process of supplying bespoke illustration.

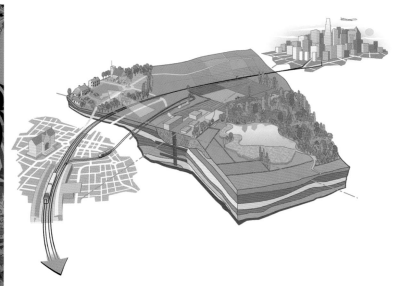

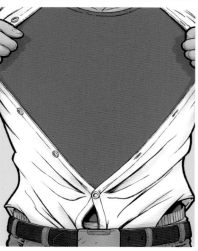

Steve Rawlings

Début Art & The Coningsby Gallery
30 Tottenham Street
London W1T 4RJ
UK

T + 44 (0)20 7636 1064
T + 44 (0)20 7636 7478
F + 44 (0)20 7580 7017
E info@debutart.com
W www.debutart.com

Steve's beautiful and highly textural compositions attract connoisseurs of the photo-illustrative art form worldwide in advertising, design and publishing. Steve conducts his own photography and can also work with client supplied material.

Previous clients include: Diageo (UDV Classic Malt Whiskies), BP, Honda, Volkswagen, The Royal Opera House, NCR, LucasFilms (USA), Scholastic/ Disney (USA), Random House (UK and USA), Harper Collins (UK and USA), Kenco, NASDAQ, 3i plc, NTT Telecom, The LSE, NatWest Bank, Orion Publ., Penguin Books, New Scientist, The FT.

Further examples of Steve's work can be found in his extensive folio on-line at www.debutart.com

the coningsby gallery

Cover commission for book 'Anastasia' by Vladimir Megre.

Book cover commission from Random House (USA).
'Roots and Wings' by Many Ly.

Book cover commission from Orion Books.
'The Margarets' by Sheri S. Tepper.

Book cover commission from Pearson Education.
'Cry, Thy Beloved Country' by Alan Paton.

Début Art Image Stock Library

30 Tottenham Street
London W1T 4RJ
UK

☎ + 44 (0)20 7636 1064
☎ + 44 (0)20 7636 7478
📠 + 44 (0)20 7580 7017
✉ info@debutart.com
🌐 www.debutart.com (click Stock Library bar)

The Début Art Image Stock Library comprises literally 1000's of top quality, high resolution illustrations that are available for immediate re-use. All images in the library have been created over the last 25 years by the leading illustrators promoted by Début Art Ltd. All images can be emailed at high-resolution directly to clients. To review the images go to the 'Stock Library' bar on the home page of www.debutart.com. All images are keyworded/searchable by medium, style and type of content. If changes/revisions are desired to any of the images the illustrator who created the original image is available to make the changes. All images in the library are the © of the image-maker who created the image originally. In-media image re-sale rights are reserved by the image creator.

the coningsby gallery

Candy Lab Limited. 130 Shaftesbury Avenue, London W1D 5EU

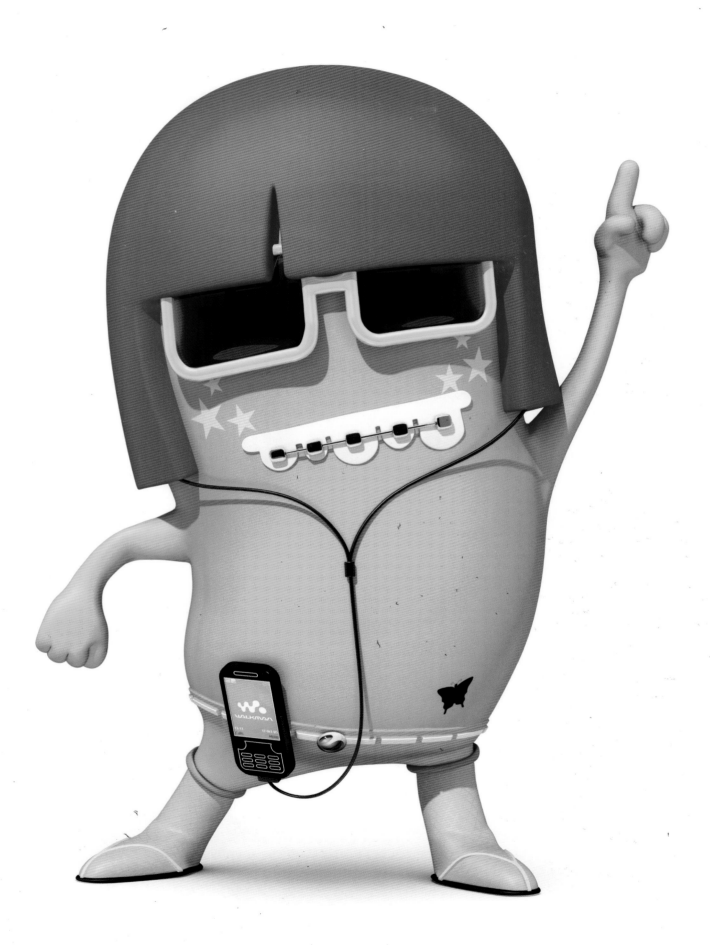

CandyLab

Candy Lab Limited. 130 Shaftesbury Avenue, London W1D 5EU

CandyLab

costelao

smith

brodner

jay jay

bollinger

pp

bernasconi

caparo

yucel

morrow

balbusso

go to the pros

santat

haya

koelsch

heinemier

a.k.a.

pickering

raven

holder

salamunic

short

bowman

dibley

shroades

jade

baez

phillips

john jay

keltie

gordon

faricy

trudel

heinemier

spector

spork

nielsen

gabor

moon

rivas

white

CONTACT
QUICK REFERENCE THUMBNAIL CATEGORY INDEX

The following categorised sections present thumbnail crops of images on the main pages in the book. Browse through these to find artists who work on specific subjects, media or genre.

Each thumbnail image has details of the artist and the page their work appears on. The online version of these pages has click through links from thumbnail image to main page where more work and full contact details can be found as well as links to email and web addresses.

Please note that not every illustrator has chosen to include their work in a category, so you will find more illustrators of every style within the main pages of the book. E&OE.

The categories included are as listed here:

3D/Assemblage, Sculptural

Third Edge Ltd
Page 203

Peter Hutchinson
Page 204

Bill Ledger
Page 209

Digital Progression
Page 342

Animals, Zoological, Botanical & Nature

Alan Baker
Page 20

Janice Nicolson
Page 24

Andy Hunt
Page 25

Emily Bolam
Page 29

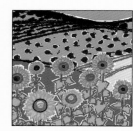

Sarah Kelly
Page 83

John Haslam
Page 84

John Haslam
Page 84

Maltings Partnership
Page 90

Maltings Partnership
Page 91

William Donohoe
Page 114

Alan McGowan
Page 150

Simon Roulstone
Page 186

Sarah J Coleman
Page 213

Fred van Deelen
Page 218

Jo Brown
Page 231

Bryan Ceney
Page 266

Ian Mitchell
Page 268

Gary Redford
Page 276

Gary Redford
Page 276

Gary Redford
Page 276

Lesley Wakerley
Page 280

Animation & Character Design

Andy Hunt
Page 25

Andrew Hennessey
Page 37

Jane Massey
Page 45

Ronald Kurniawan
Page 53

Kenneth Andersson
Page 61

Andrew Painter
Page 78

Serge Seidlitz
Page 81

George Onions
Page 97

Kathy Wyatt
Page 117

Sam McCullen
Page 174

Studio Liddell
Page 177

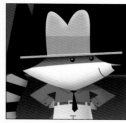

Bill Ledger
Page 209

Espresso Animation
Page 241

Finger Industries
Page 250

Dylan Gibson Illustration
Page 254

Anthony Rule
Page 262

Caroline Jayne Church
Page 294

Arlene Adams
Page 308

Uwe Mayer
Page 309

Cartoon, Humour & Caricature

Andy Hunt
Page 25

Kate Taylor
Page 26

Colin Shelbourn
Page 30

Pete Ellis
Page 36

Andrew Hennessey
Page 37

Derek Matthews
Page 49

Andrew Painter
Page 79

John Haslam
Page 84

John Haslam
Page 84

Piers Baker
Page 85

George Onions
Page 97

Tony Healey
Page 115

David Banks
Page 116

The Comic Stripper
Page 126

Satoshi Kambayashi
Page 161

Richard Levesley
Page 166

Kevin O'Keefe
Page 175

Bill Ledger
Page 209

Glen McBeth
Page 228

Glyn Goodwin
Page 240

Espresso Animation
Page 241

Paul Cemmick
Page 245

Ned Jolliffe
Page 252

Russ Tudor
Page 263

Caroline Jayne Church
Page 294

Uwe Mayer
Page 309

Jamie Sneddon
Page 315

Richard Merritt
Page 321

Children's Books & Illustration

Paul Morton
Page 11

Jon Higham
Page 12

Andy Hunt
Page 25

Emily Bolam
Page 29

Julie Clough
Page 31

Debbie Clark
Page 35

Andrew Hennessey
Page 37

Jane Massey
Page 45

Jane Massey
Page 45

Nick Hardcastle
Page 55

Jacquie O'Neill
Page 86

George Onions
Page 97

Eric Smith
Page 99

Mark Beech
Page 118

Gabriella Buckingham
Page 124

The Comic Stripper
Page 126

Adrienne Salgado
Page 128

Andres Martinez Ricci
Page 129

Alex Steele-Morgan
Page 130

Angela Swan
Page 131

David Dean
Page 132

Carol Liddiment
Page 133

Beccy Blake
Page 141

Nicola Streeten
Page 144

Sam McCullen
Page 174

Sarah J Coleman
Page 212

Chris Davidson
Page 214

Deborah Van De Leijgraaf
Page 216

Ingela Peterson Arrhenius
Page 217

Richard Johnson
Page 220

Children's Books & Illustration continued

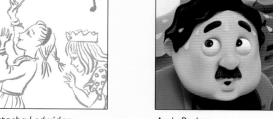

Natacha Ledwidge
Page 221

Andy Parker
Page 229

Jo Brown
Page 231

Annabel Tempest
Page 234

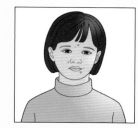

Annabel Milne
Page 237

Alison Jay
Page 243

Mark Ruffle
Page 244

Javier Joaquin
Page 247

Ruth Rivers
Page 248

Sophie Rohrbach
Page 249

Robin Edmonds
Page 264

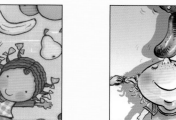

Caroline Jayne Church
Page 294

Leo Broadley
Page 302

Arlene Adams
Page 308

Uwe Mayer
Page 309

Genny Haines
Page 313

Richard Merritt
Page 321

Lynn Heaton
Page 322

Duck Egg Blue
Page 324

NB Illustration
Page 341

Collage & Mixed Media

Paul Garland
Page 19

Caroline Tomlinson
Page 50

Miles Cole
Page 54

Matthew Cooper
Page 88

Martin O'Neill
Page 121

Collage & Mixed Media continued

Conceptual

Diagrammatic, Medical & Cartographic

Hemesh Alles
Page 22

Emily Bolam
Page 29

Mike Ritchie
Page 44

Paul Shorrock
Page 73

Jane Smith
Page 138

Nicola Streeten
Page 144

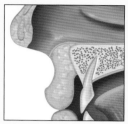

Simon Roulstone
Page 186

Peter Hutchinson
Page 204

Annabel Milne
Page 236

Annabel Milne
Page 237

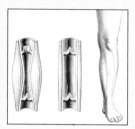

Annabel Milne
Page 237

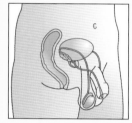

Annabel Milne
Page 237

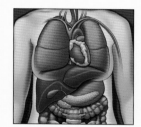

Myles Talbot
Page 260

Myles Talbot
Page 260

Ian Mitchell
Page 269

Digital, Flat Colour, Graphic

Ben Morris
Page 17

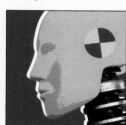

Paul Garland
Page 19

Gary Bullock
Page 21

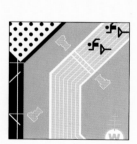

Creative Eye Illustration
Page 46

Bryan Holdaway
Page 48

Nick Hardcastle
Page 55

Evelina Frescura
Page 62

Alex Trochut
Page 75

ilovedust
Page 76

Sarah Kelly
Page 83

Digital, Flat Colour, Graphic continued

Jacquie O'Neill
Page 86

Hawaii
Page 111

Matthew Dartford
Page 112

Andy Baker
Page 125

Jane Smith
Page 139

Chris Mitchell
Page 142

Chris Mitchell
Page 143

Sophie Toulouse
Page 148

Sally Newton
Page 157

Sarah Jones
Page 158

Carol del Angel
Page 160

Lucy Oldfield
Page 165

Anthony Pike
Page 172

Neil Webb
Page 191

Red Mist
Page 195

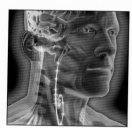

Oliver Burston
Page 199

Paul Oakley
Page 222

Barry Downard
Page 233

David Whittle
Page 246

Javier Joaquin
Page 247

Dylan Gibson Illustration
Page 254

Redseal
Page 267

Gary Redford
Page 276

Gary Redford
Page 276

Peter Crowther Associates
Page 285

Flatliner V2
Page 287

Rowena Dugdale
Page 292

Arlene Adams
Page 308

Uwe Mayer
Page 309

Gary Newman
Page 318

Digital, Flat Colour, Graphic continued

Gary Newman
Page 318

Gary Newman
Page 318

Gary Newman
Page 319

Laurence Whiteley
Page 339

The Long & the Short of it
Page 355

Editorial

Janette Bornmarker
Page 9

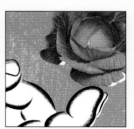
Paul Garland
Page 19

Robin Howlett
Page 82

Sarah Kelly
Page 83

Jacquie O'Neill
Page 87

Cameron Law
Page 96

Bernice Lum
Page 135

Jane Smith
Page 139

Maria Taylor
Page 159

Samara Byran
Page 164

Sam McCullen
Page 174

Tim Ellis
Page 181

Kath Walker Illustration
Page 187

Kath Walker Illustration
Page 187

Kath Walker Illustration
Page 187

Kath Walker Illustration
Page 187

Robyn Neild
Page 188

Lorna Siviter
Page 219

Dylan Gibson Illustration
Page 254

Ian Mitchell
Page 268

Editorial continued

Uwe Mayer
Page 309

Jamie Sneddon
Page 315

Gary Newman
Page 318

Gary Newman
Page 318

Gary Newman
Page 318

Gary Newman
Page 318

Fantasy & Science Fiction

Hemesh Alles
Page 22

The Comic Stripper
Page 126

Sarah J Coleman
Page 213

Figurative, People

Hemesh Alles
Page 22

Joy Gosney
Page 28

David Axtell
Page 39

Martin Handford
Page 42

Jane Massey
Page 45

Figurative, People continued

Creative Eye Illustration
Page 46

Nick Hardcastle
Page 55

Jacky Rough
Page 58

Christina K
Page 59

Evelina Frescura
Page 62

Sarah Kelly
Page 83

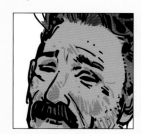

Jacquie O'Neill
Page 87

Maltings Partnership
Page 90

Maltings Partnership
Page 91

Jerry Hoare
Page 94

Clare Nicholas
Page 100

David Manktelow
Page 102

Patrick Morgan
Page 106

James Taylor
Page 109

Kathy Wyatt
Page 117

James Carey
Page 123

Annie Boberg
Page 134

Jane Smith
Page 139

Alan McGowan
Page 150

Saeko
Page 151

Stephen Elford
Page 156

Sally Newton
Page 157

Graham Humphreys
Page 162

Anne Cakebread
Page 168

Brian Gallagher
Page 182

Kate Miller
Page 184

Kath Walker Illustration
Page 187

Kath Walker Illustration
Page 187

Robyn Neild
Page 188

Arno
Page 197

Figurative, People continued

Marina Caruso
Page 205

Domanic Li
Page 215

Simon Farr
Page 235

Annabel Milne
Page 236

Dylan Gibson Illustration
Page 254

Jill Calder
Page 255

Myles Talbot
Page 260

Myles Talbot
Page 261

Gary Redford
Page 276

Paul Bateman
Page 288

Arlene Adams
Page 308

Uwe Mayer
Page 309

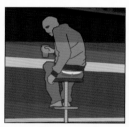
Jamie Sneddon
Page 315

Gary Newman
Page 319

Gary Newman
Page 319

Gary Newman
Page 319

Richard Merritt
Page 321

Alexander Beeching
Page 325

Karen Donnelly
Page 334

John Batten
Page 346

Packaging & Informational Design

Gary Bullock
Page 21

Creative Eye Illustration
Page 46

Creative Eye Illustration
Page 47

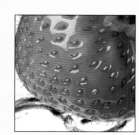
www.fruitman.com
Page 51

Ronald Wilson
Page 103

Packaging & Informational Design continued

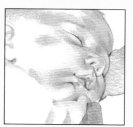
Kathy Wyatt
Page 117

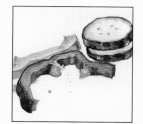
Alan McGowan
Page 150

Studio Liddell
Page 176

Mathew Hall
Page 189

Fred van Deelen
Page 218

Octagon Comp. Graphics
Page 238

Graham Evernden
Page 242

Graham Evernden
Page 242

Graham Evernden
Page 242

Graham Evernden
Page 242

Myles Talbot
Page 261

Gary Redford
Page 276

Gary Newman
Page 318

Jacques Fabre
Page 338

Photo illustration

Maltings Partnership
Page 91

Vault49
Page 105

Studio Liddell
Page 177

Sarah Howell
Page 179

Nick Reddyhoff
Page 194

Third Edge Ltd
Page 202

Vincent Wakerley
Page 206

Jackdaw
Page 211

Octagon Comp. Graphics
Page 238

Paul Bateman
Page 288

Photo illustration continued

Kerry Roper
Page 297

Jamie Sneddon
Page 316

Steve Rawlings
Page 364

Technical/Engineering & Architectural

Creative Eye Illustration
Page 47

Maltings Partnership
Page 90

Maltings Partnership
Page 91

Maltings Partnership
Page 91

Stephen Conlin
Page 92

William Donohoe
Page 114

Studio Liddell
Page 177

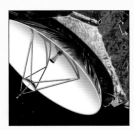

Simon Roulstone
Page 186

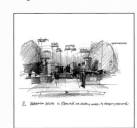

Peter Hutchinson
Page 204

Chris Davidson
Page 214

Octagon Comp. Graphics
Page 238

Myles Talbot
Page 261

Gary Redford
Page 276

Short
Page 304

Jamie Sneddon
Page 314

John See Illustration
Page 344

Traditional Media

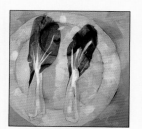

Christopher Jasper Rainham
Page 16

Vince McIndoe
Page 140

Paul Catherall
Page 163

Peter Hutchinson
Page 204

Fred van Deelen
Page 218

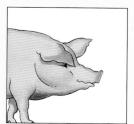

Fred van Deelen
Page 218

Pat Thorne
Page 281

Typographic, Calligraphic

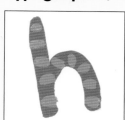

Emily Bolam
Page 29

Andy Smith
Page 153

Per Karlen
Page 171

Kath Walker Illustration
Page 187

Kath Walker Illustration
Page 187

Sarah J Coleman
Page 212

Ian Mitchell
Page 269

Gary Redford
Page 276

Richard Merritt
Page 321

ILLUSTRATORS INDEX

Everyone in this book is a member of the
Contact A Creative website and their details
and more samples of their work can be found at:
www.contactacreative.com

Everyone in this book is a member of
Contact A Creative *and their details and
more samples of their work can be found at:*
www.contactacreative.com

CREATIVES IN CONTACT

www.**contact**-uk.com

*creatives in contact **world-wide***